D1539928

AMERICAN POLICY OF RECOGNITION TOWARDS MEXICO

THE JOHNS HOPKINS UNIVERSITY STUDIES IN
HISTORICAL AND POLITICAL SCIENCE
Under the Direction of the Departments of History,
Political Economy, and Political Science

American Policy of Recognition

Towards Mexico

By

STUART ALEXANDER MacCORKLE, Ph. D.
Instructor in Political Science, University of Texas

AMS PRESS
NEW YORK

Reprinted from the edition of 1933, Baltimore

First AMS EDITION published 1971

Manufactured in the United States of America

International Standard Book Number: 0-404-04108-6

Library of Congress Catalog Number: 70-155620

AMS PRESS INC.
NEW YORK, N.Y. 10003

PREFACE

The author first intended to write his dissertation upon the subject of the American Recognition Policy towards Central and South American States. Such a work soon proved too extensive, and as a result it was deemed advisable to limit the scope of the study to one particular country, namely, Mexico.

No attempt is made to give an account of the diplomatic relations between the United States and Mexico from 1822 to the present date. On the other hand, an effort is made to analyze each instance in which the United States discussed the granting of recognition to a new Mexican government and to determine, if possible, the basis upon which such recognition was given or withheld. An attempt is made to determine if the United States has followed towards Mexico what might be termed a policy of recognition, and, if so, how such a policy conforms to our general recognition policy. With the exception of the first chapter, in which recognition is discussed in general, and the second chapter, where the recognition of Mexico as a new state is treated, this study deals only with the recognition of new governments.

In the preparation of this work the author has made use of a great mass of printed diplomatic documents, the correspondence between the American Ministers in Mexico and the Secretaries of State down to 1906, as well as numerous memoirs and biographies of the chief participants of the period. Since 1906, because the archives of the State Department are not yet open, greater use has been made of contemporary periodicals and newspapers. Particular attention has been given to Chapters III and IV, in which the recognition of the Juarez government and the Diaz government has been treated respectively. As far as the author knows, this is the first time the State Department has been used in obtaining material for the treatment of these two governments.

5

The writer wishes to thank Professor W. W. Willoughby, Head of the Department of Political Science of The Johns Hopkins University, and Dr. James Hart, of the same Department, for their inspiration, suggestions and valuable criticism offered during the process of this work. The author is also under obligation to the late Professor John H. Latané for his encouragement and assistance in the field of historical research. Acknowledgment must also be made to Dr. Charles C. Tansill for his suggestions and several very fruitful ideas.

S. A. M.

Baltimore, Maryland
February, 1931

CONTENTS

———

AMERICAN POLICY OF RECOGNITION
TOWARDS MEXICO

CHAPTER I

RECOGNITION

The purpose of this chapter is not to present a treatise upon the theory of recognition, for there is little which the writer can hope to add to the authoritative discussions already appearing upon this subject. However, it might be deemed profitable to restate briefly, in general terms, some of the more important principles regarding recognition in order that a clearer conception may be obtained before we approach our particular problem. It is for clarity and a better understanding of that which is to follow that the present chapter is written.

THE MEANING AND HISTORICAL DEVELOPMENT OF RECOGNITION AS A CONCEPT OF INTERNATIONAL LAW

To use Rivier's definition, recognition is "the assurance given to a new state that it will be permitted to hold its place and rank in the character of an independent political organism in the society of nations." [1] In the law of nations, much depends upon recognition. A newly organized state can gain admission to the circle of international law only when it is recognized by other states. Through recognition a "de facto" state becomes an international person and a subject of international law. Thus, in many cases, recognition becomes both useful and necessary. [2]

For a few moments let us turn to the historical development of recognition as a concept of international law. In its earliest stages the theory of recognition is seen first as a

---

[1] John B. Moore, Digest of International Law, I, 72.
[2] See Oppenheim, International Law (2d ed.), I, sec. 71; also Wheaton, International Law (Lawrence's 2d ed.), p. 38.

doctrine of a personal ruler, a doctrine "which upheld the established hereditary right of a single house against all other individual claimants." Later it developed into the principle of legitimacy of monarchy itself, and eventually it passed into a concept of the legitimacy of an established government against any opposing one.[3]

When the idea of sovereignty was severed from personality, a situation was created which furnished the necessity and practicability of recognition as a concept of international law. Goebel says that

it is at this stage that legitimacy after a brief revival of its dynastic form became a definite theory of international law, a theory of legitimacy of existing governments and states as against all changes in political form. In this sense, it was directly contrary to the principle of 'de facto-ism,' and in this form it has never ceased to reappear.[4]

The legitimist's views did not permit the recognition of changes in situations in which the normative power of facts may provide the remedy for existing evils, while the "de facto-ism" is willing to recognize this, although the legal order may be violated.[5]

One is not surprised that the decline of the old ideas concerning the legitimacy of the existing political regime should have antedated the development of the modern conception of recognition. It is clear that this change was necessary before a permanent state could recognize the establishment of new states through a recognition of a newly created political organism. Again, this alteration was necessary before there could be a valid basis for the recognition of newly created governments in states whose existence was previously acknowledged. There are those who still uphold the theory of legitimacy, yet the principles that were essential to this theory have been forced out of use by the modern state.

A state may be accorded either conditional or unconditional

[3] Julius Goebel, The Recognition Policy of the United States, in Columbia University Studies in History, Economics and Public Law, LXVI, 20.
[4] Ibid., p. 43.
[5] Ibid., p. 48.

recognition,[6] and it may either be expressly granted or implied from acts of the recognizing power.[7] In many cases recognition has been given by a group of states acting in unison,[8] yet few have been the cases in which the United States has participated in such collective action. The recognition of a state is absolute and in most cases irrevocable,[9] but the recognized state may refuse to accept it with or without conditions attached. In order to be effective it must be granted by a government which is itself recognized.[10] One should not forget to draw a distinction between recognition in the sense in which it has been used above and recognition of belligerency.[11] Recognition of belligerency " does not confer upon the community recognized all the rights of an independent state, but it grants to its government and subjects the rights and imposes upon them the obligations of an independent state in all matters relating to war." [12] Also, a distinction should be drawn between " de jure " and " de facto " recognition. A " de jure " recognition in international law means the recognition of the political group which ought to possess the powers of sovereignty at the time it may be deprived of them, while " de facto " recognition is a recognition of the political group which is really in possession of these powers, although the possession may be wrongful or uncertain.[13] The political reasons why a state may decide to grant the latter rather than the former may be obvious, yet the legal difference between them is not clear. There seems to be a tendency in international law to regard " de facto " recognition as revocable but " de jure " recognition once given as final and irrevocable. Apparently for international and municipal law the legal consequence of " de jure " recognition, and, while

---

[6] C. C. Hyde, International Law, I, 58.
[7] Moore, I, 73.
[8] Hyde, I, 58.
[9] G. G. Wilson, Handbook on International Law, p. 21.
[10] Moore, I, 73.
[11] See Hyde, I, 77-82.
[12] Moore, I, 164.
[13] See Charles G. Fenwick, International Law, pp. 108-109; also John G. Hervey, The Legal Effects of Recognition in International Law, pp. 11-12.

it lasts, of " de facto " recognition upon actual transactions with the government recognized, is the same.[14] When a state is recognized " de facto," it may enjoy all sovereign rights, but not until it has been recognized " de jure " can its exercise of them be fully assured.[15]

Writers upon International Law have attempted to draw a distinction between the recognition of a new state and the recognition of a new government in an already existing state.[16] Membership in the Family of Nations can be either original or acquired. It is original in the case of states maintaining diplomatic relations since the time international law began. States subsequently admitted to the Family of Nations must have obtained their legal personality through an act of " recognition " from the already existing members. In the case of a new government there are no legal rights possessed by the state as such, but the issue is who is to be competent to speak in the name of the state. Mr. Goebel has taken the view that the recognition of a new state is generally viewed as an act of legal importance, while the recognition of a new government is dismissed as a question of policy.[17] It seems to be generally accepted to-day that a state has a continuity of personality which is not affected by governmental changes; [18] at any rate, it is with the political organism of the state that the recognizing power has to deal. There may be a moral obligation to grant recognition, yet it is commonly conceded that no state is duty bound to accord it.[19]

As regards the responsibility of revolutionary governments,

---

[14] Oppenheim, International Law (McNair ed.), I, 158.
[15] Alphonse Rivier, Principles du Droit des Gens, I, 58; also C. A. Berdahl, " The Power of Recognition," American Journal of International Law, 1920, XIV, 519.
[16] The United States recognizes Russia to-day as a state but refuses to accord recognition to the Soviet government of that state.
[17] For a full discussion of this point see Goebel, pp. 60-68.
[18] The Sapphini (1871), 11 Wallace, 164.
[19] Hall, p. 82. ". . . though no state has a right to withhold recognition when it has been earned, states must be allowed to judge for themselves whether a community claiming to be recognized really possesses all the necessary marks, and especially whether it is likely to live "—see Moore, I, 72; also Fenwick, p. 105.

it is exceedingly difficult to say much that is definite.[20] Apparently in most cases when a government is created through a revolution, it is held responsible for the acts of the revolutionists as well as for those of the government it has displaced. Its acts are considered as those of a " de facto " government, for which the state is liable from the beginning of the revolution. Thus, the successful revolutionists are seemingly bound from the beginning of the' revolution for all unlawful acts and for national treaties, for the violation of which they are held liable as successors of the titular government.[21]

Most authorities agree that premature recognition is a wrong committed against the parent state; that it is, in effect, an act of intervention, which may properly be considered as a cause for war.[22] It becomes, therefore, of particular importance to discover where the power of recognition rests and by whom it may be exercised.

THE POWER OF RECOGNITION UNDER THE AMERICAN CONSTITUTIONAL SYSTEM

The Constitution of the United States does not expressly mention the power of recognition, nor does it delegate that power to a particular department of government. It does provide, however, that the President

---

[20] For a treatment of the responsibility of the state for the acts and obligations of local " de facto " governments and revolutionists, see Minnesota Law Review, February, 1930, pp. 251-270.

[21] Yale Law Review, XXVI, 339-340.

[22] Amos S. Hershey, The Essentials of International Public Law, p. 124. " The justice of a cause or sympathy with an oppressed people are wholly insufficient grounds of recognition either of belligerency or independence. Premature or unjustified recognition of independence is a gross affront to the parent state and practically amounts to an intervention in the internal affairs of another nation which may result in war. Such was the recognition of the independence of the United States by France in 1778, which was followed by a declaration of war on the part of Great Britain. Other examples of intervention in the guise of recognition were the recognition of the independence of Greece and Belgium by the Powers in 1827-1830, Cuba in 1898 and Panama in 1903." See Hyde, p. 67; Moore, I, 73; Berdahl's article in the American Journal of International Law, XIV, 519.

. . . shall have power, by and with the advice and consent of the Senate, to make treaties, provided two-thirds of the Senators present concur; and he shall nominate, and by and with the advice and consent of the Senate, shall appoint ambassadors, other public ministers and consuls. . . .[23]

It also makes provision that the President " shall receive ambassadors and other public ministers." [24]   Under the latter provision President Washington received M. Genêt on May 17, 1793, as the minister of the new French Republic, which was, in the words of Jefferson, " an acknowledgement of the legitimacy of their Government." [25]

The question has often been asked, whether or not the power of recognition is entirely within the hands of the Executive branch—whether it is the exclusive power of the President,[26] or whether Congress enjoys an independent or concurrent power of recognition, or whether there are circumstances that might at least require consultation with Congress before extending recognition.   In President Monroe's administration, Henry Clay, then Speaker of the House, moved that a salary be provided for a minister to the " independent province of the La Plata." [27]   Though the bill failed to pass, it showed the attitude which certain members of Congress had assumed at this date.   Congress during this early period made no claim to the right to recognize states of its own accord; yet, it did make claim from time to time that recognition might be granted indirectly through the exercise of congressional powers such as those of making appropriations and regulating commerce.[28]

---

[23] Constitution, Art. II, sec. 2, cl. 2.
[24] Ibid., sec. 3.
[25] Writings of Jefferson (Ford ed.), VI, 217.
[26] E. S. Corwin, The President's Control of Foreign Relations, p. 71. " It should be remarked that the President might appoint a minister to a foreign state during a recess of the Senate, and thus accord recognition without the consent of the Senate. . . . The necessity of a later confirmation of the appointment would not operate as a delay of recognition, nor would a refusal to confirm amount to a withdrawal of recognition—it would merely require an appointment agreeable to the Senate."
[27] American State Papers, Foreign Relations, I, 184; also 54th Cong., 2d sess., S. Doc. No. 56, p. 21.
[28] J. M. Mathews in his book entitled The Conduct of American Foreign Relations, p. 118, writes: "Although the power of Congress

The next congressional comments relative to the recognition of foreign states, after the recognition of the Latin-American states, occurred in connection with Texas. Texas maintained a body of Commissioners at Washington to present her case for some time prior to her recognition. Apparently popular sentiment was in favor of her recognition, judging from the number of petitions which came to Congress from the States. The conclusion of the first session of the Twenty-Fourth Congress found both the executive and legislative branches of our government in favor of recognition. Yet, the tendency to place the responsibility for such an act upon the President became more apparent.[29] In February of 1837, the Howard resolution directed the Committee on Ways and Means to provide an appropriation to cover the expenses of any agent the President might send to Texas. The funds were provided and congressional discussion of the matter came to an end.[30] President Van Buren soon afterwards recognized the Republic of Texas by sending a chargé d'affaires to the new government.

thus to affect recognition was not admitted by the President, Monroe, by his action, indicated, that in a matter of such importance, the cooperation and support of Congress was desirable, especially since the act of recognition might be considered a *casus belli* by Spain. The incident shows, however, that the power to recognize, as well as the responsibility for recognition rests with the President." Also read 54th Cong., 2d sess., S. Doc. No. 56.

[29] 24th Cong., 1st sess., H. Report No. 854.

[30] Congressional Globe, IV, 213. In a message to Congress in December of 1836, President Jackson in discussing the question said: " In the Preamble of the resolution of the House of Representatives it is distinctly intimated that the expediency of recognizing the independence of Texas would be left to the decision of Congress. In this view, on the ground of expediency, I am disposed to concur, and do not, therefore, consider it necessary to express any opinion as to the strict constitutional right of the Executive, either apart from or in conjunction with the Senate over the Subject. It is to be presumed that on no future occasion will a dispute arise, as none has heretofore occurred between the Executive and Legislative in the exercise of the power of recognition. It will always be considered consistent with the spirit of the constitution, and most safe, that it should be exercised, when probably leading to war, with a previous understanding by that body by whom war can alone be declared, and by whom all provisions for sustaining its perils must be furnished." Richardson, Messages and Papers of the Presidents, III, 267.

Other instances in which Congress has been inclined to claim the right of recognition, or at least to influence such action, we shall only mention. During the Maximilian intervention in Mexico, the Committee on Foreign Affairs of the House passed a resolution on December 15, 1864,[31] voicing its disapproval of foreign intervention in that country. In 1868, when Cuba was engaged in a revolution against Spain, agitation favoring recognition was evident in Congress but never materialized. The administration was subjected to pressure but refused to give recognition.[32] Again, in December of 1897, a joint resolution was recommended by the Senate Committee on Foreign Affairs with reference to the independence of Cuba.[33] In December of 1919, Senator Fall introduced a resolution urging that recognition be withdrawn from Carranza in Mexico, and in May of 1927, Senator Borah introduced a resolution directing the President to recognize the present government of Russia.[34]

Despite what might be said of the power of Congress to accord recognition, the Executive undoubtedly has exercised the power in an almost exclusive manner. That there is a legal basis for the exercise of such power we have pointed out earlier. It does not seem too much to say that, after all, recognition is a political question and that the President's power to recognize depends upon the method which he takes in such action; at most his power is limited legally by the Senate only in an indirect manner. Professor W. W. Willoughby, in speaking of this point, says:

The recognition by the United States of a status of belligerency, or the recognition of the sovereignty and independence of a foreign government are political acts, not subjected to judicial review and are performed by the President. At times the claim has been made that this power of recognition is one to be exercised at the dictations of Congress, but precedents are against the claim. It is to be presumed, however, that when the recognition of a status of belligerency or of the independence of a revolutionary government is likely to institute a *casus belli* with some other foreign power, the President will

---

[31] Cong. Globe, IV; 38th Cong., 1st sess., p. 1408.
[32] Foreign Relations, 1875, I, 8.
[33] 56th Cong., 2d sess., S. Doc. No. 231, Part VII, p. 64.
[34] Cong. Record, 67th Cong., 2d sess., p. 6945.

be guided in large measure by the wishes of the legislative branch. Upon the other hand, it is the proper province of the Executive to refuse to be guided by a resolution on the part of the legislature if, in his judgment to do so, it would be unwise. The legislature may express its wishes or opinions, but may not command.[35]

Again, let us quote from E. S. Corwin, who says:

Even if we should admit that Congress incidentally to discharging some legislative function like that of regulating commerce might in some sense 'recognize' a new State or government, the question still remains how it would communicate its recognition, having the power neither to despatch nor receive diplomatic agents. As we have said of the states of the Confederation, Congress is as to other governments both 'deaf and dumb.' Why, then, claim for it a power which it could not possibly use save in some round about and inconclusive fashion? [36]

MODES OF ACCORDING RECOGNITION

The best authorities upon international law agree that recognition of states and new governments may take place in various ways. Recognition may be accorded by the " formal declaration in a separate and independent document, or by such declaration included in a convention dealing with such matters . . ." Recognition may result when powers carry on such negotiations between each other as could only exist between independent states.[37] Again, treaty negotiations may be carried on in such a way as to result in recognition.[38] Finally, a new state or government may be recognized by the despatch of an accredited representative to it, the reception of a like agent from the same, or by the granting of an exequatur to its consul.[39] Such states as Venezuela, Uruguay, Guatemala, and the Dominican Republic were recognized in the last-mentioned manner.[40]

---

[35] Willoughby on the Constitution, 1st ed., I, 461; also read 34th Cong., 2d sess., S. Doc. No. 56.

[36] Corwin, p. 82; also see Quincy Wright, The Control of American Foreign Relations, pp. 270-271; also Moore, I, 96, 218.

[37] Ibid., p. 97.

[38] For example, the recognition of the Nanking Government in China by the United States by a tariff treaty.

[39] Clarence A. Berdahl, " The Power of Recognition " in American Journal of International Law, XIV, 519; also see Moore, I, 97, and Hershey, p. 116.

[40] 54th Cong., 2d sess., S. Doc. No. 40, pp. 6-7, 12-13.

2

The reception of an envoy from the foreign government
was the first method used by the President in according recognition to a new government. President Washington received
M. Genêt on May 17, 1793, as the official representative of
the Republic of France. This act was a recognition of the
legitimacy of the new French government.[41] Other states
recognized in this manner were Columbia in 1882, the Empire
of Brazil in 1824, Costa Rica in 1851, Nicaragua in 1849,
and Panama in 1903.[42]

One of the common methods of extending recognition to
governments that have superseded those to which our official
representatives had been accredited has been that of issuing
letters of credence to the diplomatic agent who had represented the United States during the former régime. For
proof we need only point to the recognition of numerous
French governments between 1804 and 1870.[43] The same
can be said of our recognition of the provisional government
of Russia on March 22, 1917.[44]

Cases in which the United States has extended recognition
to new states and governments by the exchange of diplomatic
representatives and by entering into treaty negotiations have
been rather numerous. Of the first class we shall list only
a few; namely, Chile and Mexico in 1822, Bolivia in 1848,
Honduras in 1853, and Haiti in 1862.[45] For the latter group
one might cite either Greece in 1837, or Liberia in 1862 as
examples.[46] Of late years the United States has generally
recognized by express declaration. For instance, Czecho-
Slovakia was first recognized as a " de facto " belligerent
on September 2, 1918, and later complete recognition was
given on April 23, 1919.[47] Jugo-Slavia on February 7,
1919,[48] Finland on May 7, 1919,[49] Esthonia, Latvia, and

[41] Berdahl, p. 521.
[42] 54th Cong., 2d sess., S. Doc. No. 40, pp. 2, 4, 5, 11, 12.
[43] For full discussion see Berdahl's article, p. 522.
[44] Foreign Relations, 1917, p. 1211.
[45] 54th Cong., 2d sess., S. Doc. No. 40, pp. 4, 6, 7, 11, 13.
[46] Idem.
[47] Communications from the State Department, January 20, 1927.
[48] New York Times, February 8, 1919.
[49] Ibid., May 8, 1919.

Lithuania on July 28, 1922,[50] were all given recognition in like manner.

THE TRADITIONAL POLICY OF THE UNITED STATES

Without a brief discussion of our recognition policy in general this chapter would be incomplete. Before the United States entered the Family of Nations at the end of the eighteenth century, the recognition of new governments had played little part as an international problem. This was due almost entirely to the fact that in the Old World the question involved was whether the Monarch or the Prince had a legal title to his throne, or in other words, the question of dynastic legitimacy and the divine right of kings After the establishment of the United States and the changes of government in France following the Revolution of 1789, the United States took the position that it was not concerned with the question of how a new government came into existence, even though it might be a breach of the principle of legitimacy. Our Government regarded such questions as being purely domestic in nature. We only asked whether there was a responsible agency in control of the state capable of transacting business with other nations.

Thomas Jefferson is indisputably the founder of our policy of recognition. His idea of " de facto " recognition was a natural outgrowth of his notion of popular sovereignty and the right of revolution.[51] His advocacy of the recognition of " de facto " governments was based upon the assumption that those governments represented the will of the majority of people concerned. He was not interested in " de facto " governments erected by minorities.[52]

Jefferson emphasized the popular sanction of " de facto " governments as an integral part of American policy of recognition, and this influence has been felt from his day to this.

---

[50] Ibid., July 1, 1922.
[51] John H. Latané, A History of American Foreign Policy, pp. 84-85.
[52] See Jefferson's instructions to Gouverneur Morris with reference to the revolutionary government of France, November 7, 1792. Writings of Jefferson (Washington ed.), III, 489.

President Monroe was quick to press into use the " de facto " principle when he welcomed the Spanish-American States into the Family of Nations in 1822. Henry Clay reiterated this policy in the Report of the Committee of Foreign Relations on the recognition of Texas, June 18, 1836.[53] James Buchanan, as Secretary of State under President Polk, in defining the attitude of the United States towards the revolutionary government established in France in 1848, declared that we had always recognized the actually existing governments.[54] Again, in 1851, when it was necessary to restate our policy towards the French Government, Daniel Webster, Secretary of State under President Fillmore, wrote to our Minister in France:

From President Washington's time down to the present day it has been a principle always acknowledged by the United States, that every nation possesses a right to govern itself according to its own will, to change institutions at discretion, and to transact its business through whatever agent it may think proper to employ. This cardinal point in our policy has been strongly illustrated by recognizing the many forms of political power which have been successively adopted by France in the series of revolutions with which that country has been visited.[55]

It seems quite apparent from what has been said that for the first half of our national existence emphasis was certainly placed upon the " de facto " principle of recognition, but to say that with the coming of President Lincoln's Secretary of State, Mr. Seward, there was a sharp departure from the established policy for a period of twenty-five years, after which we again reverted to the " de facto " principle, is no doubt an over-statement of fact.[56] Perhaps a more correct statement of policy would be to say that during the first fifty years of the nineteenth century our State Department seemed inclined to follow the " de facto " principle; that Secretary Seward and his immediate successors pursued a

---

[53] 24th Cong., 1st sess., Sen. Doc. No. 406, p. 1.
[54] 30th Cong., 1st sess., Sen. Ex. Doc. Nos. 51-64, VII, 53.
[55] Moore, I, 126.
[56] Charles C. Tansill, " War Powers of the President of the United States with Special Reference to the Beginning of Hostilities," in Political Science Quarterly, March, 1930, XLV, 1-55.

slightly different course based upon the theory that the will of the nation is deemed to be inseparable from, or identical with, the will of the people—that is, the fact of control by the new government must appear to be accepted by " organic law with the solemnities which would seem sufficient to guarantee " its stability and permanency;[57] that beginning with 1877, to the present day, stress has been placed upon the recognized government's ability and disposition to adhere to international obligations.[58]

In many cases circumstances have dictated policy and have determined to a great degree where emphasis is placed. On September 8, 1900, Mr. David J. Hill, Acting Secretary of State under President McKinley wrote to Mr. Hart, United States Minister at Bogota, in the following manner:

The policy of the United States, announced and practiced upon occasion for more than a century, has been and is to refrain from acting upon conflicting claims to the *de jure* control of the executive power of a foreign state; but to base the recognition of a foreign government solely upon its *de facto* ability to hold the reins of administrative power. When, by reason of revolution or other internal change not wrought by regular constitutional methods, a conflict of authority exists in another country whereby the titular government to which our representatives are accredited is reduced from power and authority, the rule of the United States is to defer recognition of another executive in its place until it shall appear that it is in possession of the machinery of state, administering government with the assent of the people thereof and without substantial resistance to its authority and that it is in a position to fulfill all the international obligations and responsibilities incumbent upon a sovereign state under treaties and international law. When its establishment upon such a *de facto* basis is ascertained, it is recognized by directing the United States representative formally to notify its proper minister of his readiness to enter into relations with it, and thereafter by the still more formal means of receiving and issuing new credentials for the respective diplomatic agents.[59]

---

[57] Diplomatic Correspondence, 1866, II, 630.

[58] President Hayes, in speaking of the recognition of the Diaz Government in Mexico, said: ". . . the custom of the United States, when such revolutionary changes of government have heretofore occurred in Mexico, to recognize and enter into official relations with the 'de facto' government as soon as it should appear to have the approval of the Mexican people and should manifest a disposition to adhere to the obligations of treaties and international friendship, . . ." Moore, I, 148.

[59] Ibid., p. 139.

Later, in 1911, Mr. Philander C. Knox, Secretary of State under President Taft, voiced practically the same opinion:

Mr. Knox informs Mr. Furniss that if he is satisfied that the government of General Leconte is in full possession of the machinery of government with the acquiescence of the people of Haiti and is in a position to meet the international responsibilities he is authorized to enter into full relations with it, and that he may so inform the Haitian minister for foreign affairs.[60]

Were one to believe Mr. Henry Lane Wilson, the American Minister to Mexico during the Huerta régime, the action of President Wilson in not recognizing the Huerta Government " amounted to a complete reversal of our traditional policy of non-interference which was announced by Franklin Pierce and adhered to by every President from Pierce to Wilson." [61] As a matter of fact, it does not appear that President Wilson withheld recognition from Huerta solely because of the manner in which he obtained national power, judged by the former's ideas of what constitutional government should be, but the traditional tests of popular approval and ability to fulfil international obligations were also applied to the Mexican military leader.

An attitude similar to that of President Wilson towards violent changes of government was expressed January 25, 1926, in an informal letter to Señor Castillo, Nicaraguan Minister at Washington, from Secretary Kellogg:

The object of the Central American countries with which the United States was heartily in accord, was to promote constitutional government and orderly procedure in Central America and those Governments agreed upon a joint course of action with regard to the non-recognition of governments coming into office through *coup d'état* or revolution. The United States has adopted the principle of that Treaty (General Treaty of Peace and Amity, signed February 7, 1923) as its policy in the future recognition of Central American Governments, as it feels that by so doing it can best show its friendly disposition towards and its desire to be helpful to the Republics of Central America.[62]

There are incidents in our history, no doubt, where it can

---

[60] Foreign Relations, 1911, p. 290.
[61] Tansill, p. 33.
[62] Conference on Central American Affairs, Washington, December 4, 1922—February 7, 1923, pp. 228-229.

be pointed out that we have strayed from the principle of strict " de facto " recognition. On the other hand, our State Department has always endeavored to make it clear that there is a broad distinction between " de facto " and " de jure " recognition. The Government of the United States has been willing to grant recognition " de facto," if the new governments desiring such were based upon popular approval and if they could fulfil their international obligations. The question as to whether the " de facto " government was a legitimate one has been outside the scope of our policy of recognition.[63] The refusal of the United States to recognize a government as a " de jure " government is well illustrated by the case of Serbia in 1903.[64]

It seems as though the " de facto " doctrine is inseparable from our foreign policy. At the same time, be it remembered that the United States of the early twentieth century is not the United States of the early nineteenth. Then a young, weak nation, groping about amidst the intrigues and deceit of international diplomacy, we intuitively held to the " de facto " doctrine. At that time most of the situations involving recognition had been brought about by the same ideals that had brought our republic into existence; hence, it was not surprising to see the United States in full accord with similar movements in other localities. The United States of the twentieth century is a world power with spheres of interest everywhere. Consequently, we are now able to pursue a bolder and more indefinite policy, if we so desire. As a matter of fact, this is exactly what we have done. In the light of what has just been said, we are better able to understand the recent attitude of our State Department towards Nicaragua and Russia.[65]

---

[63] To illustrate this point, see the memorandum from Mr. Alvey A. Adee, Acting Secretary of State in the absence from Washington of Mr. Olney. This memorandum was written with reference to the recognition of the Principality of Trinidad. Olney Papers, July 30, 1895, Library of Congress.

[64] Despatches to Serbia, State Department, vol. I. Mr. Jackson to Mr. Hay, June 29, 1903.

[65] George D. Moyer, Attitude of the United States towards the

Confronted with such practices as have been last mentioned it becomes extremely difficult to generalize in regard to our recognition policy.   One is sometimes skeptically inclined to believe that we, at last a world power, are beginning to mold our diplomacy as such, and hence will treat each new case of recognition upon grounds of expediency and national interests.

With these general statements in mind as regards our policy of recognition, let us now turn to the particular problem of Mexico.

Recognition of Soviet Russia, p. 71.   Thesis, University of Pennsylvania, Philadelphia, 1926.

327.73072 M137a

C. 1

CHAPTER II

HISTORICAL BACKGROUND AND FIRST RECOGNITION

Spain governed the country to the south of us for a long period of years. Her empire, of which Mexico was a part, was comprised at first of possessions in South America, Guatemala, Yucatan, the Spanish West Indies, Florida, and the Southwest, as well as the Philippines. This empire was governed by the Council of the Indies sitting at Seville, Spain. Not until 1821 were the Spanish-American colonies successful in their revolt against the mother country, a revolt which terminated in their self-government and independence. This revolution not only had a marked bearing upon European politics, but its influence was also strongly felt in the United States, as we shall see in the pages that follow.

The causes of the Spanish-American revolt cannot be explained as the chemist explains a reaction by a formula. In each case it seems that the first cause of the uprising was not a desire for independence or a hostility to Spanish rule, but a longing to prevent Napoleon from seizing the colonies as he had seized Spain. The popular motive at first was purely patriotic and anti-French.[1] That the movement later became anti-Spanish was due to causes which had little or no part in the original uprisings.

It is clear that among the conditions which later made the revolution in Spanish America possible was a conviction entertained by some colonists that the burdens of the colonial régime were unendurable.[2] Then, too, the Spanish officials often displayed a disregard for the humane provisions of the antiquated laws of the Indies. As in the case of the English colonies in North America, the revolution in Spanish America was partly due, no doubt, to the lack of a well managed colonial system. For an intellectual cause, we should recall the spread of revolutionary doctrines which were flowing

---

[1] Latané, pp. 169-170.
[2] John H. Latané, Diplomatic Relations of the United States and Spanish America, p. 12.

25

freely from France at this time. And lastly, Spanish-American independence was influenced at least partly by the merchants of Liverpool and Manchester. With the establishment of commercial houses in the large South American cities and the permanent investment of foreign capital, it became only a question of time before these houses and this capital would play an important rôle in politics.

Professor John H. Latané says, " The maladministration of Spain's colonies may be summarized under the heads: (1) acts of oppression against the native Indian race, and (2) regulations of a commercial and political character, which acted in restraint of the economic and social development of her own offspring in America." [3]

The general account of this chapter may be applied to any one of the South American States of this early period; yet it will be in order to give at this point a short discussion dealing particularly with Mexico. In 1808, the Viceroyalty of Mexico stretched from the Isthmus Tehuantepec northward to the British possessions. This Viceroyalty was composed of twelve provinces, its capital being Mexico City, which was situated in a beautiful valley on the central plateau. This metropolis was the residence of the Viceroy and of the Mexican Archbishop, as well as the capital of the province of Mexico.[4]

The first struggle for independence in Mexico began about 1809, and was carried on at intervals until 1817. The second revolution broke out in 1820, when news was received from Spain of the revolution of March, 1820, and the reestablishment of the constitution of 1812.[5] Perhaps a cause for the first revolt in Mexico was the liberal spirit of the new rulers of Spain, rather than their oppressive acts. The Cortes elected in accordance with the Constitution of 1812 met in July of 1820, and attempted to remedy the desperate financial situation. Oppressive taxes were reduced, the deficit

---

[3] Ibid., p. 11.
[4] William S. Robertson, Rise of the Spanish American Republics, p. 73.
[5] Latané, Dip. Rel. of the U. S. and Sp. Amer., p. 52.

being made up by suppressing religious orders and confiscating a part of the church property. As a result of these actions, the Mexican clergy became alarmed and the leadership of the highest ecclesiastics formed a conspiracy which led to Iturbide's Proclamation of the " Plan of Iguala," the first article of which stated that the religion of New Spain should be " the Roman Catholic Apostolic, without tolerating any other." [6]

At first it seemed that Iturbide's prospects for success were anything but certain. Later his forces were joined by various military leaders of high rank throughout the country, and by July of 1821, most of New Spain was under his control with the exception of the cities of Mexico, Acapulco, Vera Cruz, and the fortresses of Pevote and San Juan de Utura. When the new Viceroy General, O'Donoju landed at Vera Cruz the latter part of July, he was unable to proceed inland because of the lack of an adequate military force. His first act was to issue a proclamation urging the revolting people to await the action of the Spanish Cortes, assuring them that autonomy would be granted. As a matter of fact the insurgents had autonomy; so there was little left for O'Donoju to do save treat with them. Negotiations were at once opened with the revolutionary leaders and within forty-eight hours after O'Donoju's meeting with Iturbide, a paper was signed which was later known as the Treaty of Cordova.[7] It was dated August 24, 1821, and provided that the independence of Mexico should be recognized by Spain; that the form of government should be constitutional monarchy; and that the crown should first be offered to the male members of the Spanish family in succession, but that if they declined to accept, then the Mexican Cortes should be free to name its own ruler. Both O'Donoju and Iturbide were made members of the junta.

Apparently O'Donoju had exceeded his instructions in treating with Iturbide, for the Spanish troops refused to

---

[6] George L. Rives, The United States and Mexico, I, 36.
[7] Ibid., p. 37.

recognize the validity of the Treaty of Cordova, yet they will-
ingly obeyed his orders to embark for Spain.[8] This evacuation ended Spanish rule in Mexico.

A provisional junta composed of thirty-six members who
owed their nomination to Iturbide met in Mexico City on
September 28, 1821, and appointed O'Donoju, Iturbide and
three others regents of the empire with power to govern
until an emperor was chosen. Provision was also laid down
for a Congress to be composed of two houses, and a date was
designated for the holding of preliminary elections. In the
meantime, the junta took complete control of all legislative
matters. They authorized the appointments of diplomatic
agents to the various South American States, the United
States, England, and Rome, but made no attempt to establish
diplomatic relations with the other European powers.

Upon the death of O'Donoju, Iturbide became President
and General-in-Chief of the army. Congress at once passed
provisions that no member of the regency should hold a military office. The immediate result was an uprising in Mexico
City, which terminated in Iturbide's being proclaimed Emperor by a congress which was forced to act against its
wishes.[9] An election soon followed, which chose Iturbide
with the title of Augustin I.[10] Thus, from outward appear-
ances, the new government in Mexico had been established by
popular consent. It should be remarked that the election
was held under threats of a mob and the outcome might have
been easily contested; nevertheless, the country accepted its
results, or, at least, did not revolt against them.

Mexico, having thus secured her independence and established a form of government, needed only the recognition by
other powers to enable her to take her place in the Family of
Nations. There were, however, many difficulties in the way
of such action.

We have alluded to the fact that, during the Napoleonic

[8] Ibid.
[9] Rives, p. 38.
[10] Annals of Cong., 17th Cong., 1st sess., p. 2099.

wars, there had been considerable revolutionary activity among the Spanish colonies in America, but it was not until the year 1811, when the declaration of Venezuelan independence had been announced and recognition demanded, that the first definite political steps were taken by the United States.[11] We made the Venezuelans no promises, though we did give them a conciliatory reply. The attitude of our government was disclosed by Secretary of State Monroe to Joel Barlow, who was at that time United States minister to France. A part of Barlow's instructions were as follows:

The ministers of the United States in Europe will be instructed to avail themselves of suitable opportunities to promote their recognition by other powers. You will not fail to attend to this object, which is thought to be equally due to the just claims of our Southern Brothers, to which the United States cannot be indifferent, and to the best interest of this country.[12]

In his message of November 5, 1811, President Madison drew the attention of Congress to the situation in Latin America, and indicated what he thought should be the course of the United States:

An enlarged philanthropy and an enlightened forecast concur in imposing on the National Councils an obligation to take a deep interest in their [the South American States] destinies, to cherish reciprocal sentiments of good will, to regard the progress of events, and not to be unprepared for whatever order of things may be ultimately established.[13]

This message was referred to a committee, which reported in the form of a public declaration, stating that Congress looked with friendly interest on the establishment of sovereignties by the Spanish provinces in America; that as their neighbor the United States felt a great interest in their welfare; and that when they should demonstrate their ability to fulfil national requirements, the Senate and House of Representatives would gladly stand with the Executive in establishing with them treaties of amity and commerce.[14]

At this time, two events occurred which postponed the

[11] See Instructions to U. S. Ministers in Mexico, VII, 183 (James Monroe to Joel Barlow, Am. Min. to France, November 27, 1811).
[12] Ibid., p. 183.
[13] Richardson, Messages and Papers of the Presidents, I, 491-496.
[14] American State Papers, Foreign Relations, III, 538.

question of recognition for five or six years. First was the rapid reconquest of Venezuela by Spanish troops, which put an end to the revolutionary movement there until the year 1819. The second event was the outbreak of war between the United States and Great Britain, which held the undivided attention of the former.

From the very beginning of the Spanish American revolt, the principal continental powers of Europe were opposed to an early recognition of the independence of any of Spain's former colonies. Their policy after the fall of Napoleon had been reactionary. Under the leadership of Metternich, they tried to create a coalition for the purpose of suppressing revolutionary disorders everywhere. In 1823, France, acting as the agent of the continental powers, invaded Spain, disposed of the liberal government, which had been in existence from the time of Riego's rebellion in January of 1820, and reestablished Ferdinand as an absolute monarch. But this was the last effort of which the coalition was capable. The powers failed to agree over Greece, and they were further divided in regard to a policy over Spanish Colonies. The Holy Alliance would have been willing to have given some material aid to Spain in her struggle had England consented, but when the latter refused to help, they did little save protest.

The notice for the renewal of the agitation for the recognition of the Spanish American Colonies came with the declaration of independence of the United Provinces of Rio de la Plata on July 19, 1816. Since 1810, this State had maintained a "de facto" independence under a junta, and had vigorously sought freedom.

The trend of events in South America looked so favorable to the cause of the colonies that, by October, 1817, President Monroe deemed it proper to despatch a commission of inquiry to South America and particularly to Buenos Aires and Chile.[15] The views of the commissioners differed in many

---

[15] This commission consisted of: Caesar A. Rodney, John Graham and Henry M. Brackenridge. See Am. St. Pap., For. Rel., IV, 217.

respects, and when their report was transmitted to Congress in November and December of 1818, it was composed of several different opinions.[16] Henry Clay, who had been a ready champion for the struggling colonies for a period of ten years, again came to their rescue. On March 25, 1818, in a speech before the House, he attempted to show that the United States had already established a policy of acknowledging a " de facto " government without regard to its legitimacy, pointing out that our policy towards the revolutionary governments of France proved this fact conclusively. He maintained that our duty to ourselves bound us to recognize the independence of La Plata, which possessed an organized government and an unmolested independence of eight years' duration. In conclusion, he urged the coordinate right of Congress in recognition, holding it proper for either Congress or the President to take the initial step.[17]

The following year President Monroe, in his third annual message of December 7, 1819, stressed the attitude and policy of the United States towards her struggling neighbors. He said:

In the Civil War existing between Spain and the Spanish provinces in this hemisphere, the greatest care has been taken to enforce the laws intended to preserve an impartial neutrality. Our ports have continued to be equally open to both parties and on the same conditions, and our citizens have been equally restrained from interfering in favor of either to the prejudice of the other. The progress of the War, however, has operated manifestly in favor of the colonies. Buenos Aires still maintains unshaken the independence which it declared in 1816, and has enjoyed since 1810. Like success has also lately attended Chile and the provinces north of the La Plata bordering on it, and likewise Venezuela.

This contest has from its commencement been very interesting to other powers, and to none more so than the United States. A virtuous people may, and will, confine themselves within the limit of a strict neutrality; but it is not in their power to behold a conflict so vitally important to their neighbors without the sensibility and sympathy which naturally belongs to such a case. It has been the steady purpose of this government to prevent that feeling leading to excess, and it is very gratifying to have it in my power to state

---

[16] Moore, I, 81.

[17] Calvin Colton, The Life and Times of Henry Clay (2d ed., New York, 1846), I, 216; or, Annals of Congress, 15th Cong., 1st sess., II, 1474-1500.

that so strong has been the sense throughout the whole community
of what was due to the character and obligations of the nations that
very few examples of a contrary kind have occurred.[18]

Before taking the final step, Europe was again sounded
upon the subject. In August of 1818, a circular was sent to
the European governments by the State Department for the
purpose of obtaining expressions in regard to immediate
recognition of the revolting colonies. "France," wrote Gallatin, "would view a recognition with disfavor, because of
the peculiar nature of her family ties with Spain; but she
would not fight over this cause."[19] Russia would not fight
alone, was Campbell's statement in regard to the situation
there.[20] Great Britain, to whom a formal proposal was made
for a concerted and immediate recognition of the independence of Buenos Aires, declined to accept the proposal, giving
as her only reason for refusal that it did not then suit her
policy.[21] But, it should be remarked that during Napoleon's
invasion of Spain, the British policy became more intelligible.
She thought it better to withhold recognition from the
colonies, in order that Spain might be turned against Napoleon, rather than grant them independence which would
only serve to draw the two opposing countries close together.
In the meantime British commerce continually increased
with the South American States. This being the state of
affairs, England was satisfied to allow things to drift.[22]

Thus, while the United States was concerning herself with
political interest of the Spanish Provinces, Great Britain was
reaping most of the commercial advantages. However, Clay
was not satisfied to let matters rest as they were. On April
4, 1820, he moved in the House an appropriation for an outfit and salary for such minister or ministers as the President
might, with the concurrence of the Senate, send to any of
the South American governments. This motion was carried

[18] Richardson, II, 58, 59.
[19] Despatches, State Department, France, Gallatin to Adams,
November 5, 1818.
[20] Ibid., Campbell to Adams, December 22, 1818.
[21] Moore, I, 82.
[22] See Latané, A History of American Foreign Policy, p. 174.

by a majority of five, but nothing further came of it.[23] At the next session, Clay renewed his efforts in behalf of recognition. A motion for an appropriation was defeated, but a motion was carried by which it was declared:

... that the House participates with the people of the United States in the deep interest which they feel for the success of the Spanish provinces of South America, which are struggling to establish their liberty and independence, and that it will give its constitutional support to the President whenever he may deem it expedient to recognize the Sovereignty and independency of any of the said provinces.[24]

Mr. Poinsett's report [25] emphasized that the struggle for independence in Mexico had triumphed before his arrival and that Spain had been unable to recover possession of the territory and had withdrawn all troops. He emphasized the fact that Mexico was a country of great wealth and population, and that she had been serving under Spanish rule long enough. Furthermore, it would be of a great commercial advantage for the United States to recognize Mexico as an independent nation.[26] There was no doubt as to Iturbide's power, for he had been highly successful in a military way, and his plans for the establishment of an independent government were complete.[27]

In brief, it appears that before according recognition to Mexico, the United States took into consideration many factors. Mexico was widely separated from Spain, a distance which not only marked them as different kingdoms, but, at that date, as almost belonging to two different worlds. When a nation arrives at the age when she no longer needs assistance and is able to act for herself, it is quite natural that she should refuse to depend upon others. Mexico, it seems, had reached this stage of self-support. She had shown signs of refinement,

---

[23] Annals of Cong., 16th Cong., 1st sess., II, 1781, 2229, 2230.
[24] See ibid., 16th Cong., 2d sess., pp. 1071, 1077, 1081, 1092.
[25] Mr. Poinsett was appointed by the United States' Government to investigate conditions in Mexico prior to the recognition of that country by our Government.
[26] Annals of Cong., 17th Cong., 1st sess., p. 1395.
[27] Ibid., p. 2099.

culture, and in physical qualities, such as arms and population, she was not lacking.[28]

Don Manuel Torres [29] pointed out that if the United States
should recognize Mexico there would be no conflict in prod-
ucts between the two nations. Furthermore, such an act
would enable America better to withstand and perhaps coun-
teract the Holy Alliance in Europe and to protect, to a better
advantage, our republican institutions.

We have seen that the Government of the United States
was hesitant to make the final move. It tried to preserve
neutrality, " to leave the parties to themselves," and it dili-
gently collected information as to the strength and stability
of the new government.[30] In message after message, Monroe
reiterated his determination to maintain neutrality and to
recognize the independence of the Spanish colonies, when,
but only when, the facts of independence were convincingly
established. It was not until March 8th, 1822, that the
President thought the time had come to recommend to Congress that steps should be taken to enable him to appoint
diplomatic representatives to the former Spanish colonies.
As Congress was much in advance of the President on this
subject, the measure recommended was passed without serious
delay, and became a law May 4, 1822. The following is a
part of the President's message to the House of Representatives, March 8, 1822:

When we regard then, the great length of time which this war has
been prosecuted, the complete success which has attended it in favor
of the provinces, the present conditions of the parties, and the utter
inability of Spain to produce any change in it, we are compelled to
conclude that its fate is settled, and that the provinces which have
declared their independence and are in the enjoyment of it ought
to be recognized.[31]

In 1822, one hundred thousand dollars were appropriated

---

[28] Ibid., II, 1395-1403.
[29] Am. St. Pap., For. Rel., IV, 835, Manuel Torres, Agent and
Chargé d'Affaires of the Republic of Colombia in the United States.
[30] British and Foreign State Papers, I, 1219-1222; also, Paxson,
The Independence of the South American Republics, pp. 110-118.
[31] Am. St. Pap., For. Rel., IV, 818, Monroe's Message to the House,
March 8, 1822.

for such missions to the independent nations of the American continent as the President of the United States should deem proper.[32]   When the Spanish minister in Washington heard that the President was planning to recognize Mexico, he wrote to J. Q. Adams, expressing his surprise at such steps being taken by the United States and stating that there was no government in Mexico, no pledge of stability, and no proof that the Province would not return to Spain.[33]

Adams, in his reply to Señor Anduaga, expressed the desire of the United States to keep on friendly terms with Spain, and said that heretofore his government had always adopted a policy of impartial neutrality, but that the Civil War between Spain and Mexico had ceased and that treaties had been signed between the Viceroys of Spain and the Commanders of Mexico.[34]   It was called to the attention of the Spanish Minister that, should the United States recognize Mexico as an independent nation, it would be merely the acknowledgment of existing facts, and that it was her moral obligation to do so; that such an act would add to the happiness and welfare of Spain; and that the time had come when all European governments, friendly to Spain, and Spain herself, should acknowledge the independence of the American nations.[35]

To quote: " The effect of the example of one independent nation upon the councils and measures of another can be just only so far as it is voluntary; and as the United States desires that their example should be followed, so it is her intention to follow that of others upon no other principle." [36]   By recognizing the colonies President Monroe did not intend to invalidate any right of Spain, nor to affect the employment of any means which she might have used with the view of reuniting her revolting provinces.

---

[32] Ibid., p. 850; also Annals of Congress, 17th Cong., 1st sess., II, 2603-2604.
[33] Ibid., March 9, 1822, IV, 845. Mr. Anduaga to Mr. Adams.
[34] Between the Lieut. General of the Spanish armies and Iturbide, October 24, 1821.
[35] Am. St. Pap., For. Rel., April 6, 1922, IV, 846.
[36] Ibid., p. 846.   (At this time several of the South American Republics had recognized the independence of Mexico.)

On December 12, 1822, Adams presented Zozoya to President Monroe as envoy extraordinary and minister plenipotentiary from the Mexican Empire. This ceremony constituted the formal acknowledgment of the independence of Mexico by the United States.[37]

Up to this point, the action of the United States had far outstripped that of the other nations, but, in respect to Mexico, at least, a series of delays now began. Monroe hesitated to perform a positive act of recognition.[38] He delayed the appointment of a minister to Mexico City. Finally, after about one year, Jackson was selected for the post, but Jackson, in a rather cool note, declined the offer.[39] Almost another year passed, and then Ninian Edwards' nomination was sent in to the Senate. Edwards' appointment was confirmed, but before leaving for his post he resigned the office on grounds unconnected with Mexico.[40] Monroe's next choice was Joel R. Poinsett, of South Carolina.

Poinsett had traveled widely. He had visited Europe, Siberia, and the interior of Russia, where he declined to enter the services of the Czar. He was well qualified for the position to which he was appointed and seems to have been one of the United States' best representatives in South America. His actual appointment was delayed for a time due to the presidential campaign then in progress. Not until after Adams was inaugurated were his credentials and instructions prepared. These he was unable to present officially to the Mexican President until the first of June, 1825.[41]

Henry Clay, in his instructions to Poinsett, first American minister to Mexico, impressed upon the latter the importance of this mission. Being the first minister appointed to the Mexican government by any country save those of South America, he was cautioned to be careful and to encourage

---

[37] William R. Manning, Early Diplomatic Relations Between the United States and Mexico, p. 12.
[38] Writings of James Monroe (Hamilton ed.), VI, 211.
[39] William R. Manning, Early Diplomatic Relations Between the United States and Mexico, pp. 35-37.
[40] Ibid., pp. 38-42.
[41] Ibid., pp. 43-52.

amity, commerce, navigation, and to attempt to arrange a treaty settling the boundary between the two countries. Also, he was instructed to bring to the notice of the Mexican government the fact that the American continents were not henceforth to be considered as subject to future colonization by any European powers. To give Clay's exact words, " . . . while we do not desire to interfere in Europe with the political system of the allied powers, we should regard as dangerous to our peace and safety any attempt on their part to extend their political system to any portion of this hemisphere, for the political systems of the two countries are essentially different and should be kept separated." [42]

Poinsett found it a difficult matter to conclude a treaty with Mexico which would embrace the two points of commerce and of boundaries with that promptness which his government desired, because the marking out of limits had not been finished and a vast extent of country was unexplored. For this reason, and also because a treaty of amity, commerce, and navigation would remain in force only a short time, he decided to conclude this before negotiating a treaty in regard to limits. [43] Mexico desired that the United States grant her the most favored nation clause, which was at first refused on the ground that should a war occur between the United States and any of the Spanish American countries, it would place us in an awkward position. Finally, after a long discussion, our plenipotentiary yielded the point, and the Treaty of Amity, Navigation and Commerce was signed by Poinsett in July, 1826. [44]

Clay's instructions to Poinsett had been to further our boundary, if possible, but, if such could not be obtained, to accept the boundary as stated in the treaty with Spain of February 22, 1819; also to insert a clause that each country should restrict the Indians within its territory from disturbing and violating the rights of humanity. [45] On January 12,

---

[42] Instructions to United States Ministers in Mexico, X, 227.
[43] Am. St. Pap., For. Rel., VI, 583.
[44] Ibid., p. 583; also see Inst. to Am. Min. in Mex., X, 387, on this point.
[45] Am. St. Pap., For. Rel., VI, 578.

1828, a Treaty of Limits was concluded which fixed the same boundary between Mexico and the United States as that found in the treaty named above, and both countries agreed to control the Indians within their boundaries.[46] However, neither the Treaty of Amity, Navigation and Commerce nor the Treaty of Limits was considered by Mexico until April 5, 1832, when after much discussion and threatening on the part of the United States, the Mexican government finally consented to accept them as binding.[47]

Perhaps Clay well summed up our early relations with Mexico when he said:

The United States have neither desired nor sought to obtain for themselves, in their commercial relations with new states, any privileges which were not common to other nations; that the United States was ready to extend to Mexico any favor that she extended to other nations, and that she expected a perfect reciprocity.

He continued:

There is a striking inconsistency in the line of policy which the United Mexican States seem to pursue towards the United States. They regard the United States sometimes as an European nation to be excluded from the enjoyment of privileges conceded to other American nations. But when an attack is imagined to be menaced by Europe upon the independence of Mexico an appeal is made at once to the maternal sympathies of the United States.[48]

It was not long after Monroe had recognized Mexico as an independent state until Canning, the English minister, saw fit to follow suit.[49] In fact, the British diplomatic representative arrived in Mexico City one day before the arrival of Poinsett. This was a significant step on the part of Great Britain, for it was " Canning's bid for South American support against that of the United States, and his method of breaking the ring-fence Monroe had sought to set up." [50] Again, England's recognition of the South American powers

---

[46] 25th Cong., 1st sess., H. Doc. No. 42, p. 28.
[47] Ibid., p. 28.
[48] Am. St. Pap., For. Rel., VI, 581.
[49] For an account of the Canning-Rush episode see Moore, VI, 386-392; Latané, Amer. For. Pol., p. 187; and Writings of Monroe (Ford ed.), VI, 323.
[50] Ward and Gooch, Cambridge History of British Foreign Policy, II, 73-78.

would serve a blow to France in America should she conquer Spain in Europe. Reinforced by a popular sympathy such as existed in the United States, the commercial interests made themselves felt in the Parliamentary opposition to the ministry, convincing Canning at length that they, rather than the legitimist principles of Europe, should be the object of his solicitude. To protect them, he was forced to take the first steps in recognition, which the logic of events forced him, as soon as might be, to follow to the end. It thus may be said that he called the new world into existence because he was forced to do so.[51]

In conclusion, Monroe's action was the first recognition accorded the South American States by one of the Family of Nations. It was a challenge of the new world to the old world's principle of legitimacy. In sharp contrast with the philosophy of the Congress of Vienna and the Holy Alliance, it announced to the world the principle of American foreign policy that a people should be entitled to choose their own form of government and that, having chosen and established it, they would receive the recognition of the United States. Clay's unsuccessful effort to force the hand of the executive showed where the real power of recognition lay in the American constitutional system. Yet, when Monroe was ready for the step, the United States not only welcomed the new republics into the Family of Nations, but helped insure them against further European vengeance.

---

[51] The other governments of Europe still under the reactionary influences preferred to follow the lead of Spain rather than that of England, and recognition was in most cases long delayed. Ultimately, however, it was conceded. Treaties were entered into with several of the German States, Denmark, and the Netherlands, in 1827, and with France, in 1830. Spain herself yielded with the death of Ferdinand VII, when young Isabella reigned in his place. Among the most reluctant sovereigns to face the fact of the successful rebelling colonies was the Pope. Yet, at last even the Holy See itself relented, after Spain had consented by treaty to recognize the independence of Mexico. A Mexican envoy, who had been knocking at the Vatican gates for several years in vain, was officially received by Pope Gregory XVI in 1837, and a representative from the Vatican was promised to Mexico.

CHAPTER III

A Period of Military Anarchy and Reform

This work does not permit a full treatment of the period dating from 1823 to 1860, nor is such necessary to our purpose. No other era in United States history can claim so many happenings between the two countries. The entire period was marked by the rise and fall of many a military leader, each of whom seized the government by force and ruled almost single handed until another more powerful than he appeared upon the scene, assumed governmental power and forced the former ruler to abdicate or flee from the country.

The duration of civil war not only affected the internal conditions of Mexico, but it was also destined to cause trouble in her external relationships. During the thirty-seven years the United States withdrew her diplomatic representatives only three times, and each withdrawal was noticeable for its brevity. When consideration is given to the numerous changes in government which occurred during the period, and the character of the rule of each, one is amazed that the diplomatic ruptures between the two countries were so rare.

First, let us consider the break of diplomatic relations with Mexico due to her failure to settle claims made by American citizens. No sooner had Poinsett set to work to negotiate a commercial treaty than he was beset on all sides with constant complaints from United States ship owners, whose vessels and cargoes were being seized on all sorts of pretexts by Mexican officials. Tariff rates in Mexico were varied to meet revenue needs without regard for published rates under which shipments had originally been made. Frequent revolutions necessitated constant declarations of blockade, and this state of affairs made possible a great many seizures of United States vessels on grounds of contraband or breach of a blockade which no one had known to exist. The disorder in Mexico left American travellers and merchants at the mercy of bandits, and the police sent out by the Mexican government were given to as much plundering as the robbers themselves. Due to these conditions, claim after claim piled up against Mexico, which afforded bones of contention between the two countries throughout this period.[1]

The United States government kept account of the damages done to the property of its citizens in Mexico, and periodically presented bills for their payment. In return, Mexico claimed, as she has ever since, that she had given as much protection to American citizens as she had to her own people. This statement is hard to believe, for she neither protected her own citizens nor their property rights. In other words, the United States demanded more protection for American rights than Mexico had shown herself able or disposed to give to her own citizens.

Anthony Butler, who was appointed to succeed Poinsett in 1829 as chargé d'affaires, renewed the expression of grievances and remonstrated against the unfriendly conduct of the Mexican Republic towards American property and lives.[2] Matters dragged on. The United States, time and time again, appealed to the Mexican government for redress, but with no satisfactory reply. Each attempt met with a refusal on the part of Mexico to examine the claims existing between the two countries. On January 29, 1836, Secretary Forsyth instructed Mr. Ellis, newly appointed chargé d'affaires in Mexico, to insist that the Minister of Foreign Affairs at least make an apology for neglecting to examine the existing claims.[3] Again Mexico disregarded the desires of the United States.

The accumulation of complaints on the part of American citizens against the Mexican government continued, and the disposition of that government to inquire into them, or to grant satisfaction for them, apparently decreased. Finally, on July 20, 1836, Secretary of State Forsyth expressed the

[1] See Manning, pp. 256-275, for a more detailed discussion; also Justin H. Smith, The War with Mexico, I, 58-81; Jesse S. Reeves, American Diplomacy under Tyler and Polk, pp. 28-58.
[2] Instructions to Ministers in Mexico, VI, 149-171.
[3] Ibid., pp. 15, 65.

attitude of the President upon the matter in a letter to Mr. Ellis, as follows: " He is satisfied, however, that further delay in the acknowledgment if not in the redress of the injuries complained of, cannot be acquiesced readily with the dignity, rights, and interests of the United States." [4] Forsyth continued:

If, contrary to the President's hopes, no satisfactory answer shall be given to this just and reasonable demand within three weeks, you will inform the Mexican government that unless redress is afforded without unnecessary delay, your further residence in Mexico will be useless. If this state of things continues longer, you will give formal notice to the Mexican Government that unless a satisfactory answer shall be given within a fortnight, you are instructed to ask for your passports, and, at the end of that time, if you do not receive such answer, it is the President's direction that you demand your passports and return to the United States, bringing with you the archives of the legation.[5]

Ellis acted as instructed, but not until the following December. For about three years the United States was without a Minister in Mexico City.[6]

Mexico was, however, now ready to act. Mr. Martínez was sent as minister to Washington in the spring of 1837, with instructions to enter into a treaty agreement for the referring of the existing claims to arbitration.[7] The United States met Mexico's advance, and relations were soon restored as a result. After much disputing, Forsyth and Martínez agreed to arbitrate the claims in a treaty concluded April 11, 1839.[8] Claims were awarded the United States, but after a few installments of the interest the Mexican government failed to make its payments. In 1843, an attempt was made to organize another commission to continue the work of the first, but that too failed.[9]

THE RECOGNITION OF TEXAS

The Texans early realized that the support of the United

---

[4] Ibid., p. 75.
[5] Ibid., p. 80.
[6] See 24th Cong., 2d sess., H. Ex. Doc. No. 139; also S. Doc. No. 160.
[7] 25th Cong., 3d sess., H. Ex. Doc. No. 252.
[8] Ibid.; also see Instructions to American Ministers, Mexico, XV, 116-117.
[9] 30th Cong., 1st sess., S. Doc. No. 52, p. 74.

States was essential to their cause. On November 12, 1824, a commission consisting of Stephen F. Austin, Branch T. Archer, and William H. Wharton was sent to Washington to work for the recognition of the new state.[10] The United States was slow to act. During a greater part of Jackson's administration,[11] neither he nor Henry Clay[12] appeared to favor the recognition of Texas' independence.

On March 3, 1836, appropriations were made by Congress for an outfit and salary for an Envoy Extraordinary and Minister Plenipotentiary to Texas, whenever the President of the United States should receive satisfactory evidence that Texas was an independent power, and when he should deem it expedient to appoint such a minister.[13]

Later, on June 18, 1836, Mr. Clay introduced the following resolution in the Senate:

Resolved, that the independence of Texas ought to be acknowledged by the United States whenever satisfactory information shall be received that it has in successful operation a civil government capable of performing the duties and fulfilling the obligations of an independent power.[14]

Nearly one year later the independence of Texas was recognized by the appointment of Mr. Alcie La Branche as chargé d'affaires to that Republic.[15] The State Department now used almost the same argument to justify its actions that it had used at an earlier date in regard to the independence of Mexico.[16]

---

[10] Ethel Z. Rather, Recognition of the Republic of Texas by the United States. The Quarterly of the Texas State Historical Association, January, 1910, XIII, 167.

[11] Richardson, III, 265-269, Jackson's Message of Dec. 21, 1836.

[12] 24th Cong., 1st sess., S. Doc. No. 406, pp. 1, 2.

[13] United States Statutes at Large, V, 170.

[14] 54th Cong., 2d sess., S. Doc. No. 56, p. 41.

[15] Instructions to Ministers, Texas, I, 1. Mr. Forsyth, Secretary of State, to Mr. La Branche, May 21, 1837.

[16] Notes to the Mexican Legation, VI, 71. Mr. Forsyth to Señor Castillo, March 17, 1837. To quote, "The independence of other nations has always been regarded by the United States as a question of fact merely and that of every people has been invariably recognized by them whenever the actual enjoyment of it was accompanied by satisfactory evidence of their power and determination permanently and effectually to maintain it. This was the course pursued by the

Let us briefly consider the Texas question from another point of view.

WAR WITH MEXICO

The next minister to be appointed to Mexico after the recall of Ellis was Waddy Thompson, late in March of 1842.[17] His stay only lasted about two years, for in the summer of 1844 he resigned and Wilson Shannon was at once named in his place.[18] On March 29 of the next year Shannon was recalled and William S. Parrott was sent as a secret agent to Mexico with instructions to attempt to convince the Mexican authorities that the United States was ready to meet all unsettled questions between the two countries in a liberal and friendly manner, and that a minister would be sent to Mexico as soon as assurances were given that he would be received.[19] On November 9, 1845, Parrott reported to the State Department the willingness of Mexico to receive an American envoy.[20]

When John Slidell reached Mexico City on a special mission early in December 1845,[21] the situation had become critical between the two countries. Slidell's instructions reviewed the question of claims and Mexico's disregard of the demands of the United States. He was informed: " The fact is but too well known to the world that the Mexican government is not now in a condition to satisfy those claims by payment of money." [22] It is evident that the United States was willing to assume the claims of its citizens if Mexico would agree to a satisfactory adjustment of the Rio Grande boundary. The overthrow of the Herrera Government in 1846 and the temporary establishment of General Paredes did not tend to cause a change in the outcome of

---

United States in acknowledging the independence of Mexico and the other American States, formally under the dominion of Spain. . ."
[17] George L. Rives, The United States and Mexico, I, 509.
[18] Ibid., p. 661.
[19] Ibid., p. 702.
[20] Ibid., II, 67-68.
[21] Ibid., p. 71.
[22] 30th Cong., 1st sess., S. Ex. Doc. No. 52, p. 78.

events. The new ruler assumed a position of hostility towards the United States and swore to defend all Mexican
territory, including the whole of Texas. The United States,
having determined that the question of Texas was settled, and
that territorial indemnity must be offered in settlement of
the American claims, had resolved that war must follow if
Mexico refused to treat on this basis. Further assurance of
this is found in the fact that the receipt of Slidell's first
despatch, telling of his nonreception on January 12, 1846,
was followed the next day by orders to General Taylor at
Corpus Christi to move forward to the Rio Grande. This in
itself was not an act of war, but the presence of the United
States troops on the Rio Grande meant that either the Mexican government would heed the threats and receive the
American minister or hostilities would ensue.

On March 1, 1846, when Slidell applied to Castillo, the
Foreign minister of the Paredes government, for recognition,
he was rebuffed, the objection being the attitude of the United
States in regard to Texas and the military and naval movements already undertaken. In the meantime Secretary of
State Buchanan wrote to Slidell directing him to remain in
Mexico until the Oregon question was settled. " Your return to the United States before the result is known would
produce considerable alarm in the public mind, and might
possibly exercise an injurious influence upon our relations
with Great Britain." [23]

Buchanan's instructions had been prepared some time before they were sent, probably just after the cabinet meeting
of February 17 in which the President had urged that Slidell
be directed again to press his application, and if again rebuffed, to go aboard an American warship, from which he
would demand the immediate payment of American claims. If
this demand should be ignored the President would call upon
Congress to cause Slidell to make a final demand, and " if
this was refused by Mexico, to confer authority on the

[23] Buchanan to Slidell, March 12, 1846, John B. Moore, (ed), The
Works of James Buchanan, VI, 402.

Executive to take redress into our hands by aggressive measures." [24]

From what has been said, it is evident that Polk intended tó declare war on Mexico if she refused to receive our minister, but that he wished to delay the act if possible until the Oregon matter was settled. The President even went so far as to instruct Slidell to inform the Paredes government that the United States was both able and willing to relieve his administration from pecuniary embarrassment if he would do us justice and settle the question of the boundary between the two countries. [25]

All hope of settlement perished when word came from Slidell on April 7 that the Paredes government had again refused to receive him and that he was on the way home. President Polk thereupon advised the cabinet that he would call upon Congress " for legislative measures and take the remedy in our own hands." It was decided to delay this action until Slidell should present himself, but to act against Mexico regardless of the status of the Oregon question. When Slidell arrived, in reply to his advice for war, Polk replied that he had decided to communicate with Congress on the matter.

Polk and the cabinet agreed to declare war on Mexico May 12, 1846. Bancroft said he " should be better satisfied if the Mexicans had, or should, commit any act of hostility." He was destined to be satisfied, for that evening news of the skirmish of April 24 near Matamoros, in territory claimed by the United States, reached Washington, thus enabling Polk in the message to Congress submitted on May 11, to say, " War exists by the act of Mexico."

While the skirmish at Matamoros was the occasion for the declaration of war by the United States, it is evident from the facts given that the true cause was somewhat deeper. As we have seen, Polk was prepared to declare war, before the skirmish occurred, for the reason that Mexico refused to re-

---

[24] Polk's Diary, February 17, 1846.
[25] 29th Cong., 1st sess., S. Doc. No. 337, Buchanan to Slidell, March 12, 1846; also, see Reeves, pp. 294-295.

ceive our minister sent to adjust the American claims by the method of territorial indemnity. Mexico's reason for this refusal was based upon the refusal of the United States to discuss the political status of Texas, the question which had caused the break of diplomatic relations between the two. We have, then, as the fundamental causes of the Mexican war, the inevitable and perhaps legitimate expansion of the United States on the one hand and the condition of civil war in Mexico on the other.

Even after war was declared, it was only for a short time that our country was without a minister in Mexico City. Trist, being appointed early in 1847, was clothed with diplomatic powers although his true mission was supposed to be to conclude a treaty of peace between that country and the United States.[26]

Finally, Trist succeeded in concluding a treaty of peace between the Mexican government and that of the United States which was signed at Guadalupe Hidalgo February 2, 1848, thus bringing the war to an end.

The war left Mexico in a sad state. The money she received from the United States did not benefit her in her disorganized condition; neither did the victory of the United States settle the boundary disputes between the two countries. The line of the Rio Grande was well marked, but the southern boundary of New Mexico and the line of the Gila were to produce five years of disagreement and negotiation. The result was another treaty in 1853, whereby the United States paid Mexico ten million dollars for another strip of her territory. As usual, Santa Anna was in need of cash and was only too glad to dispose of the land. The United States paid the sum not only to settle the boundary, but also in order to acquire a southern route for a Pacific railway. Santa Anna defended this additional loss of territory on the ground that the United States would have taken it anyway.[27]

---

[26] 30th Cong., 1st sess., S. Doc. Vol. 7, February 23, 1848; also read ibid., November 24, 1847.

[27] P. N. Garben, The Gadsden Treaty, pp. 83-92; also see J. Fred Rippy, chs. vi, vii, and viii.

THE LATER FIFTIES

In 1857, a favorable change occurred in Mexican affairs. A federal republican constitution was framed and adopted by a constituent congress, the members of which were chosen by the people of the different states. Under this constitution an election was held in July of 1857, and General Comonfort was chosen President with little opposition. His term of office was to last for four years beginning December 1, 1857. Within a month he was driven from power and a military government was established under the leadership of General Zuloaga. Civil war soon broke out again between the reactionaries led by Zuloaga and the republicans who were directed by Benito Juarez. Zuloaga was soon disposed of, being succeeded by Miguel Miramon. The latter was overthrown and General Benito Juarez, the President of the Supreme Court of Justice, became "de jure" President of the Republic.[28]

General Zuloaga was recognized by the American minister without waiting for instructions from the State Department at Washington. As a matter of fact, there was no answer from the State Department to the despatch in which Mr. Forsyth reported this action.[29] When Zuloaga was expelled

---

[28] See Moore, I, 146, 147.

[29] Moore, History and Digest of International Arbitrations to which the United States has been a Party, II, 1289. Despatches from the Ministers, Mexico, Vol. 21, Despatch No. 66. John Forsyth to Lewis Cass, January 29, 1858: "The question of recognizing the new government has occupied my serious and anxious attention. My colleagues of the Diplomatic body had little difficulty in determining it, and even at an early moment were unanimous in favor of its recognition. In making up my own mind I had to struggle with my natural sympathies in favor of the party which professes to stand upon a constitutional government based upon the consent of the nation. The point of inquiry to which I directed my mind in the solution of the difficulty was which is the government 'de facto.' The inquiry admitted only of a doubtful answer. The Zuloaga Government was in possession of the capital and the public archives, and claims, already, the adhesion of ten of the States, and the custom of the Diplomatic body has been to recognize the government at the Capital regardless of the status of the constitutional government, intelligence at the Capital was based solely on hearsay, and newspaper reports. According to these, Juarez, the President of the Supreme Court, upon whom devolved the Presidency of the Republic

and the supreme power was seized by General Miramon, again our Foreign Minister entered into relations with the latter without the slightest bit of delay. Meanwhile Juarez, the constitutional President, had put into operation his administration at Vera Cruz.[30]

For several months Mr. Forsyth continued to discharge his duties at Mexico City. At last the crisis came when a decree was issued by the Mexican government levying a contribution pro rata upon all the capital in the republic between certain specified amounts, whether held by foreigners or Mexicans. Mr. Forsyth regarded this decree as a "forced loan" and protested against its being applied to American citizens, at the same time advising them not to pay the contribution, but to permit it to be forcibly exacted.[31] Relations with the Miramon government had been bad for some time, but now they became unbearable because of the outrages committed against American citizens [32] and the personal indignities to Mr. Forsyth. In June of 1858, Forsyth suspended diplomatic relations between the two governments.[33] President Bu-

in the absence of the President elect was at Guanajuato, organizing a government under the constitution of 1857." It seems that at this time the Diplomatic Corps received no communication from the Juarez Government, for Forsyth said, "Had the Juarez Government communicated to me its constitutional organization and asked my recognition the case would have been difficult."

[30] Moore, Digest, I, 147.

[31] Acting upon Mr. Forsyth's advice an American citizen, Solomon Migel, refused to pay the contribution. Accordingly his property was seized by force to satisfy the amount. Not content with this action the government banished him from the country. Our minister at once made it known that if the decree should be enforced he would feel it his duty to adopt "the most decided measures that belonged to the powers and obligations of the representative office." The banishment was enforced and Mr. Forsyth promptly announced to the government the suspension of diplomatic relations between the two countries until the pleasure of his own government should be ascertained. See Rippy, ch. vii.

[32] Notes to the Mexican Legation, XVII, 201-202. Secretary of State Cass to Mr. Forsyth, July 15, 1858.

[33] 35th Cong., 2d sess., S. Ex. Doc. No. I, p. 41; also ibid., p. 48. Secretary of State, Lewis Cass, on July 15, 1858, instructed John Forsyth as follows, in regard to the government located at Mexico City:

"The government at the Capital has neglected the just complaints of the United States and evinced no disposition whatever to redress

4

chanan approved of his actions and directed him to return to
the United States, giving as a reason for this action that it
was impossible to maintain friendly intercourse with a government under whose usurped authority wrongs were constantly committed and never redressed. To quote:

We have been nominally at peace with that Republic, but so far as
the interests of our commerce, or of our citizens who have visited
the country as merchants, shipmasters, or in other capacities are
concerned, we might as well have been at war. Life has been insecure,
property unprotected, and trade impossible except at a risk of loss
which prudent men cannot be expected to incur.[34]

As we have seen, all diplomatic intercourse was terminated
between our government and that of Miramon, but none was
established with the Juarez government.[35] But the success
of the latter seemed so probable that the following year the
President despatched William M. Churchwell as a confidential
agent to Mexico for the purpose of investigating actual conditions there.[36] Mr. Churchwell sent back reports on February 8 and 22, 1859, respectively, in which he represented the

the injuries that have been committed upon the persons and property
of our citizens. Your previous efforts upon this subject have failed
and the reports received from you indicate little expectation of a
favorable change till the United States, to adopt your own language,
shall give striking evidence of their will and power to protect their
citizens. Immediately after the receipt of this despatch you will
communicate this decision to the Mexican government and request
the necessary passports for yourself and your suite. You will proceed to Vera Cruz where an armed steamer has been ordered to repair
and await your arrival. She will convey yourself and your family
and secretary to such convenient part of the United States as you
may indicate."
Notes to the Mexican Legation, XVII, 201-202. Secretary of State
Cass to Mr. John Forsyth, July 15, 1858.
    [34] Richardson, V, 565. For an account of the period dating from
1857-1860, see 45th Cong., 2d sess., H. Reports, 1877-1878, Appendix
A. Extracts from the Annual Messages of President Buchanan.
    [35] Moore, Digest, I, 147.
    [36] Notes to Mexican Legation, XVII, 205. Lewis Cass to William
Churchwell, December 27, 1858. Part of the instructions read:
" From the President's message to Congress at the opening of this
session you will have gathered the views of the Administration upon
the subject of Mexican affairs. The liberal party in Mexico has our
hearty sympathy, and we are disposed to give it any moral support
which may result from our recognition of its supremacy, whenever
such recognition can take place in conformity with our usual policy
upon such occasions."

cause of the liberal party under Juarez as steadily gaining ground, and advised that Juarez be recognized as President of the Republic.[37]   At the same time, a melancholy picture was painted of the country, over which there seemed to be little or no control. Besides favoring the liberal government, Mr. Churchwell also enclosed a memorandum signed by Juarez in which the latter agreed to cede, under certain conditions, not only lower California but also a perpetual right-of-way over Tehuantepec and from the Rio Grande to Guaymas and Mazatlan, respectively.[38]

In addition the Mexican Government agreed:

Firstly, for the settlement of all claims of citizens of the United States against Mexico.

Secondly, for freedom of trade upon principle of perfect reciprocity on all the transits, and as far as practicable in the general commerce between Mexico and the United States.

Thirdly, for the efficient protection of persons and property in transits over the same.[39]

Both Mexico and the United States agreed to prevent the hostile invasion of Indians into the territory of the other republic.

Largely on the strength of Churchwell's advice, Mr. Robert M. McLane, a new minister, was sent to Mexico, March 8, 1859,[40] " with discretionary authority to recognize the government of President Juarez, if on his arrival in Mexico he should find it entitled to such recognition according to the established practice of the United States." [41]

Secretary Cass' instructions to McLane were in part as follows:

The first question presented to you on your arrival in Mexico will be in reference to the recognition of a government there, with which you can transact business.   The general rules by which the United States have been controlled on this subject are quite familiar to you. Guided by these rules, if you find a government in Mexico, which

---

[37] Despatches from the Ministers, Mexico Dept. of St., Vol. 23, Despatch No. 1—c.

[38] Ibid., Vol. 23, Despatch No. 1—c.

[39] Mexican Instructions, XVII, 206.

[40] Ibid., XXIII, Despatch No. 1—c.

[41] Moore, Digest, I, 147.

exercises general authority over the country, and is likely to maintain itself, you will of course, recognize it, without reference to any
opinions which you may have as to the rightfulness of its existence.
The question whether there is a government in any country is not a
question of right, but of fact, and in the ascertainment of this fact
in Mexico very much must be left to your discretion. Undoubtedly,
however, the sympathies of the United States have been strongly
enlisted in favor of the party of Juarez which is now established at
Vera Cruz, and this government would be glad to see it successful.
This arises not only from the fact it is believed to be a constitutional
party, but because, also, its general views are understood to be more
liberal than those of the party opposed to it, and because, moreover,
it is believed to entertain friendly sentiments toward the United
States. Notwithstanding this preference, our government cannot
properly intervene in its behalf, without violating a cardinal feature
of our foreign policy. Yet, it would be an agreeable duty to give it
the full weight of our recognition, at the earliest period when its
condition and prospects would justify us in doing so. The single
fact that it is not in possession of the city of Mexico, ought not to
be a conclusive consideration against it. If its authority is obeyed
over a large majority of the country and the people, and is likely
to continue, it would be extremely unjust to delay an acknowledgement of it, because its opponents are in possession of the capital. On
this subject, however, your own judgment must be your best guide,
after you shall have reached your destination and shall have had
time to inform yourself of the actual condition of affairs in the
country. It is possible that before your arrival, they may have
assumed a character which will relieve you from all embarrassment.[42]

And again:

You are authorized, whenever under your instructions you shall have
recognized a government in Mexico, and shall find it willing to negotiate a satisfactory treaty of commerce and limits with the United
States, to enter upon such negotiations without delay.[43]

On April 7, 1859, Mr. McLane presented his credentials
to President Juarez, announcing his government to be the
only existing government of the republic. McLane was
cordially received by the authorities at Vera Cruz and every
effort was made by the new government to manifest a friendly
attitude toward the United States.[44] And, on April 27, 1859,
Señor Mata was presented to the President by Secretary Cass
as Envoy Extraordinary and Minister Plenipotentiary of the
Mexican Republic.[45] Recognition was now continued without

---

[42] Instructions to American Ministers in Mexico, XVII, 209-213.
[43] Ibid.
[44] For President Buchanan's version of the recognition of the
Juarez government read 45th Cong., 2d sess., H. Reports, 1877-1878,
Appendix G, p. 439.
[45] Notes to the Mexican Legation, XVII, 139, Mr. Cass to Señor
Mata, April 27, 1859.

interruption from April of 1859, until November of 1876, when the constitutional order was overthrown by the successful military revolution of Diaz.

After recounting the unstable and disturbed condition in Mexico, Mr. McLane in a communication to Secretary Cass explained his actions on the following basis:

In any other country than Mexico, I should have had grave doubts in coming to the conclusion at which I have arrived, but a view of the very large interest, political and commercial, already involved in the right of way over the Isthmus of Tehuantepec, and with the knowledge that this transit was the subject of present legislation or decrees by both governments, and that the State of Louora also which offered so desirable a route from the Pacific Ocean to our territory of Arizona, was now engaged in a contest with the central government in relation to its public domain in that state, in which contest the rights and property of American citizens were deeply involved, I felt it to be my duty to act promptly in opening political relations with some power, if such could be found consistent with those principles by which I had been instructed to govern myself.[46]

There is little doubt that the presence of English and French fleets anchored in the harbor of Vera Cruz, which demanded the performance of commercial conventions contracted with governments of Mexico, tended to hasten the action of the United States.

Mr. McLane concluded his report as follows:

I have said enough, however, to indicate fully the grounds on which was founded my judgment that it was important to open and maintain political relations with the Republic of Mexico, and that the government of President Juarez was the only government existing in Mexico that posessesed any of the substantial elements of a *de facto* government or that offered reasonable prospect of stability— that it lacks much in this latter aspect of the case, which is necessary to give full satisfaction to those with whom it may have to deal, it would be idle to deny, but, on the other hand, it is in truth the constitutional government of the Empire. President Juarez having been elected Chief Justice by the people when Comonfort was elected President two years ago, became, in virtue of his office, under the constitution President, when Comonfort abandoned the constitutional government and fled the country. It is conceded by all that he is an honest and pure man, an enlightened statesman and patriot, and I think he is well disposed in feeling and principle to the people and government of the United States. . . .

Having thus assured myself of the good feeling and friendly disposition of the government of President Juarez, and believing it to be

---

[46] Despatches from the Ministers, Mexico, XXIII, Despatch No. I, Mr. McLane to Secretary Cass, April 7, 1859.

important that political relations should be opened with some government, I resolved to waive those scruples which I entertained and have expressed in this Despatch in regard to its strength and stability, and by the tone and manner of recognition, give it the full advantage of this great moral fact, at the same time laying the foundation of a cordial and friendly intercourse in the future. Which will, if it endures, have a happy exchange for the hostile and offensive demonstrations that characterize all our relations with those who are now in possession of the city of Mexico; with whom it would be very difficult to open political relations were they ever in " de facto " possession of the government.[47]

Up to this time the United States had followed its early established principle of *de facto* recognition, influenced, it seems, by a spirit of liberalism and an intense desire for the gain of territory. In the previous history of Mexico a successful military revolution at the capital had in most cases been the signal for submission throughout the Republic. Not so in 1858-1859. A majority of the citizens sustained the constitutional government at Vera Cruz. Heretofore, the United States had recognized the various revolutionary governments as they appeared at the capital. In this instance more stress was placed upon the protection of American lives and property rights in Mexico, the settlement of claims, and the willingness of President Juarez to negotiate a satisfactory treaty of commerce and limits with the United States. In other words, our policy seems to have become less vague during the later fifties. There seems in this instance to have been a sharp departure from the traditional policy of recognition. On the other hand, never before had the State Department at Washington dwelt at such length upon the outrages perpetrated upon American citizens domiciled in Mexico before granting *de facto* recognition.

---

[47] Ibid.

CHAPTER IV

The Maximilian Government

The Civil War left several foreign as well as domestic problems for the United States to face. One of these was a dispute with England over the so-called " Alabama Claims," and another with France, because of her intervention in Mexico. It is to the latter that we are now to give our attention.

Louis Napoleon's attempt to establish an empire in Mexico under the leadership of Maximilian of Austria was a direct challenge to the Monroe Doctrine. The stimulus which led to this step on the part of Napoleon was the refusal or the inability of Mexico to meet her financial obligations. It will be recalled that in 1842 she had signed an agreement with England, France, and Spain, whereby she promised to set aside a percentage of the customs duties of Vera Cruz and Tampico in order that both the interest and principal of her indebtedness might be met. As a result of an ever changing government she had failed to meet her payments. Claims had arisen because of outrages committed on the person and property of European subjects residing in Mexico; also the amounts of the claims of bondholders were most astounding. The whole matter was brought to a climax when President Juarez in July of 1861 issued a decree suspending for two years all payment on the foreign debts.[1] At once the European powers demanded a repeal of this decree, and when Mexico refused to comply with their demands they broke diplomatic relations and began preparations for a joint military expedition.

Seward attempted to relieve Mexico to some degree from her embarrassing position. In September of 1861, he authorized the negotiation of a treaty with Mexico whereby the United States agreed to assume the interest on all foreign debts for a period of five years, the public land and mineral rights in Lower California, Chihuahua, Sonora, and Sinaloa

---

[1] 37th Cong., 2d sess., H. Ex. Doc. No. 100.

being given for security.[2] England and France, as well as the United States Senate, objected to this plan, and so it was soon dropped. But on October 31, 1861, a convention was held in London in which Great Britain, France, and Spain agreed upon joint intervention. One of the most important articles of this convention Emperor Napoleon violated later when he attempted the acquisition of the Mexican territory and government.[3]

The European powers recognizing that the United States also had claims against Mexico, asked her cooperation in dealing with the matter. Mr. Seward replied:

It is true, as the high contracting parties assume, that the United States have, on their part, claims to urge against Mexico. Upon due consideration, however, the President is of the opinion that it would be inexpedient to seek satisfaction of their claims at this time through an act of accession to the convention. Among the reasons for this decision which the undersigned is authorized to assign are, first, that the United States, so far as it is practicable, prefer to adhere to a traditional policy recommended to them by the Father of their country and confirmed by a happy experience, which forbids them from making alliances with foreign nations; second, Mexico being a neighbor of the United States on this continent, and possessing a system of government similar to our own in many of its important features, the United States habitually cherish a decided good-will towards that republic, and a lively interest in its security, prosperity and welfare. Animated by these sentiments, the United States do not feel inclined to resort to forcible remedies for their claims at the present moment, when the government of Mexico is deeply disturbed by factions within, and exposed to war with foreign nations. And of course, the same sentiments render them still more disinclined to allied war against Mexico, than to war to be waged against her by themselves alone.[4]

According to the London convention, Vera Cruz was occupied in the early part of 1862 by British, French, and Spanish forces. But the allies soon disagreed. The British and Spanish decided to adopt independent lines of action, and, coming to terms with the Mexican government, they soon ordered their forces to withdraw from Mexican territory.[5] Napoleon III refused the same terms as were offered to the

---

[2] Ibid., p. 100.
[3] Latané, A Hist. of Amer. For. Pol., p. 402.
[4] 37th Cong., 2d sess., H. Ex. VIII, 189.
[5] 37th Cong., 3d sess., H. Ex. Doc. No. 54, p. 48.

other two powers, appearing, it seems, determined to overthrow the Republic of Mexico.

Mr. Seward expressed the opinion of the United States government in a despatch to Mr. William L. Dayton, American Minister to France, dated June 21, 1862:

> France has a right to make war against Mexico, and to determine for herself the cause. We have a right and interest to insist that France shall not improve the war she makes to raise up in Mexico an anti-republican or anti-American government, or to maintain such a government there. France has disclaimed such designs, and we, besides reposing faith in the assurances given in a frank, honorable manner, would, in any case, be bound to wait for, and not anticipate a violation of them. . . . We do not desire to suppress the fact that our sympathies are with Mexico, and our wishes are for the restoration of peace within her borders; nor do we, in any sense, for any purpose, disapprove of her present form of government or distrust her administration. We may have our opinions about the necessity or the expediency of the movements of France, in regard to that power.[6]

Although the United States disapproved of French intervention in Mexican affairs, Napoleon continued to land troops. Mexico City was taken and the republican government forced to move its capitol to San Luis Potosi, where it established itself; and the two governments remained hostile towards each other. Corwin, who had been accredited to the Republic in Mexico was instructed by Secretary Seward that it would not be necessary for him to present himself to the new government then occupying Mexico City.[7]

Seward sketched the outlines of his policy in two documents to the Legations of the United States abroad. In the first, written on March 3, 1863, after the purpose of the European powers was definitely understood, he said:

> The president has relied upon the assurance given his government by the allies that they were in pursuit of no political object, but simply the redress of their grievances. He entertains no doubt of the sincerity of the allies; and if his confidence in their good faith has been disturbed, it would be restored by the frank explanations given by them that the governments of Spain, France, and Great Britain had no intention of interfering to procure a change in the constitutional form of government now existing in Mexico, or any political change which should be in opposition to the will of the Mexican people. . . .

---

[6] Ibid., pp. 530-531.
[7] Instructions to Ministers, Mexico, XVII, 452.

Nevertheless the President regards it as his duty to express to the Allies, in all kindness and candour that a monarchical government, in the presence of foreign fleets and armies, occupying the waters and soil of Mexico, has no promise of security or permanence; in the second place, that the instability of such a monarchy would be enhanced if the throne were assigned to a person alien to Mexico; that in these circumstances the new government would instantly fall unless sustained by European alliances, which would be practically the beginning of a permanent policy of armed intervention by monarchical Europe, at once injurious and inimical to the system of government generally adopted by the American continent.

These views are based upon some knowledge of the opinions and political habits of American society. There can be no doubt that in this matter the permanent interests and sympathies of our country would be on the side of the other American republics.

We must not be understood as predicting on this occasion the course of events which may ensue, both in America and Europe, from the steps which are contemplated. It is enough to say that in the opinion of the President the emancipation of the American continent from the control of Europe has been the principal characteristic of the past half-century. It is not probable that a revolution in the opposite direction can succeed in the age which immediately follows this period, and while the population of America increases so rapidly, while its resources develop in the same proportion, and while society forms itself uniformly to the principle of the American democratic government. . . .[8]

Again on March 31, 1862, Seward in his instructions to Dayton said:

You will intimate to Mr. Thouvenel that rumors of this kind have reached the President and awakened some anxiety on his part. You will say that you are not authorized to ask explanations, but you are sure that if any can be made, which will be calculated to relieve that anxiety, they will be very welcome, inasmuch as the United States desire nothing so much as to maintain a good understanding and the most cordial relations with the government and people of France.

It will hardly be necessary to do more in assigning your reasons for this proceeding on your part than to say that we have more than once informed all the parties to the alliance that we cannot look with indifference upon any armed European intervention for political ends in a country situated so near and connected with us so closely as Mexico.[9]

Such was Seward's Mexican policy as outlined in 1862. It was founded upon expediency and apparently dictated by common sense.

---

[8] Quoted from James M. Callahan, Evolution of Seward's Mexican Policy, pp. 31-32.
[9] 37th Cong., 3d sess., H. Ex. Doc. No. 100, p. 218.

On October 3, 1863, Maximilian was formally offered the Mexican crown by a deputation of citizens, but he refused to accept it unless his acceptance was confirmed by the wish of the whole nation. This refusal the archduke failed to maintain, for six months later he accepted the crown without the question having been submitted to the majority of the Mexican people.

As early as May 10, 1862, Secretary Seward instructed Mr. Thomas Corwin, American Minister to Mexico, as follows:

War, it appears, has been actually begun between France and Mexico. It is possible that it may result in an overthrow of the existing government of the republic, and the inauguration, or attempt at inauguration, of some new system. It is not the interest of the United States to be hasty in recognizing the revolutionary changes which unhappily are so frequently occurring in Spanish America. It is not safe to judge that a new government among them, under whatever auspices it may arise, will prove satisfactory to the people and become permanent. At the same time, it is neither our right nor our duty to prejudge and condemn any new constitution or administration which the fortunes of internal war may call into being. In view of these considerations, the President expects that you will suspend any definite act of recognition in case of a dynastic change in Mexico, and will refer the subject to his own consideration.[10]

No one doubts but that the chances of Maximilian's success in Mexico had from the beginning been coupled with the success of the Southern Confederacy. Thus the cause of the Juarez government and the cause of the Union came to be one. The sympathy of the Union was with the Mexican republic, yet for a while there was a doubt in the mind of the American people as to the exact purpose of France in Mexico. As to this point, Seward wrote Dayton on September 21, 1863, saying:

Owing to this circumstance, it becomes very difficult for this government to enforce a rigid observance of its neutrality laws. The President thinks it desirable that you should seek an opportunity to mention these facts to Mr. Drouyn de Lhuys, and to suggest to him that the interests of the United States, and, as it seems to us, the interests of France herself, require that a solution of the present complications of Mexico be made, as early as may be convenient, upon the basis of the unity and independence of Mexico.[11]

[10] Instructions to Ministers, Mexico, XVII, 406, Mr. Seward to Mr. Corwin, May 10, 1862.
[11] 38th Cong., 2d sess., Sen. Ex. Doc. No. 11, p. 465.

The French minister replied by declaring that the question of establishing Maximilian on the Mexican throne would be decided by a vote of the entire nation, and that the sooner the United States manifested a willingness to enter into peaceful relations with the new government, the quicker France would be able to leave Mexico, thus permitting the Archduke to take care of himself. At the same time, it was made clear to Seward that since France had sponsored the Archduke's actions she would not desert him until his government was settled.[12]

In reply, Mr. Seward mentioned the fact that the French government had been informed of the opposition of the United States to the establishment of a foreign and monarchical government in Mexico and that this opinion still remained unchanged. It was also called to the attention of Mr. Drouyn de Lhuys that the United States continued to regard Mexico as a theatre of a war which had not yet ended in the subversion of the government existing there, with which the United States remained in peace and friendship. For these reasons the United States was not at liberty to consider the question of recognizing a government which in the further chances of war, might come into its place. Furthermore, the United States consistent with her principles could only leave the destinies of Mexico in the keeping of her own people, and recognize their sovereignty and independence in whatever form they should choose to manifest it.[13]

In January of 1863, Senator McDougall, of California, introduced a resolution into the Senate which declared that French intervention in Mexico was an act of hostility against the United States, and that it was the duty of the government to meet this by a demand of immediate withdrawal of French forces. Largely due to the able leadership of Charles Sumner these resolutions met with defeat both in 1863 and 1864.[14] Seward's friends in the House did not prove so

[12] Ibid., p. 471.
[13] Ibid., p. 473.
[14] Latané, A Hist. of Amer. For. Pol., p. 408.

strong, for on April 4, 1864, Henry W. Davis put through
that body by unanimous vote a resolution declaring that it
would be contrary to accepted American policy to acknowledge a monarchy erected upon the ruins of a republican
government.[15]

The rupture that Mr. Seward had been striving so hard
to avert until after the war between the States seemed most
likely to happen. When Mr. Dayton visited Mr. Drouyn de
Lhuys just after the news of the action of the lower House
had reached France, he was addressed in this manner, " Do
you bring us peace or bring us war? " Mr. Dayton replied
that he did not think France had a right to infer that we
were about to make war against her on account of anything
contained in the resolution; that it was the executive who had
control of foreign affairs and not the House of Representatives; but that the act embodied nothing more than the principles which the United States had constantly held out to
France from the beginning.[16]

In July, 1865, Maximilian made an effort to obtain recognition of his government by the United States. On the 17th
of July, the Marquis Montholon, the French minister at
Washington, informed Mr. Seward that a special agent had
arrived in Washington with a letter from Maximilian addressed to the President of the United States. A copy of the
letter was presented to Mr. Seward, which he returned on the
18th to the Marquis saying that the United States was on
friendly terms with the republican government of Mexico,
and that the President had refused to receive either the letter
or its bearer.[17]

The reasons for refusing recognition to Maximilian were
stated by Mr. Seward to Mr. John Bigelow, American Consul
at Paris, as follows:

The presence and operations of a French army in Mexico, and its
maintenance of an authority there, resting upon force and not the
free will of the people of Mexico, is a cause of serious concern to

[15] Frederic Bancroft, The Life of William H. Seward, II, 428, 429.
[16] Dip. Cor., 1864, Part III, 76.
[17] Dip. Cor., 1865-1866, Part III, 485.

the United States. Nevertheless, the objection of the United States
is still broader, and includes the authority itself, which the French
Army is thus maintaining. That authority is in direct antagonism
to the policy of this government and the principles upon which it
is founded.

They [speaking of the United States] still regard the effort to
establish permanently a foreign and imperial government in Mexico
as disallowable and impracticable. For these reasons they could not
now agree to compromise the position they have heretofore assumed.
They are not prepared to recognize, or to pledge themselves hereafter
to recognize, any political institutions in Mexico which are in opposition to the republican government with which we have so long
and so constantly maintained relations of amity and friendship . . .[18]

With the Civil War over the tone of the United States
became more decided. On September 6, 1865, Mr. Seward
reminded the French government that the United States was
now in a position to give more attention to foreign affairs,
and that from now on relations between France and Mexico
would concern her most.[19] About this time General Schofield,
General Grant, and a number of other army officers were
insisting that the United States government intervene and
by force drive Maximilian from Mexico. Mr. Seward, attempting to hold Schofield and Grant in check, decided to
send the former to Paris on an informal mission. Seward
was supposedly serious when he said in a letter to Schofield:
" I want you to get your legs under Napoleon's mahogany and
tell him he must get out of Mexico." [20] Schofield was kept
waiting for more than two months and then sent to Paris,
where he passed his time feasting until May, 1866. To use
his own words, " The condition of the Franco-Mexican question at the time of my return from Europe gives no further
occasion for my offices in either of the ways which had been
contemplated in behalf of Mexico." [21] Seward's plan had
worked well.

Finally, on December 16, 1865, Seward addressed what
might have been termed an ultimatum to France. He stated
in part:

---

[18] Ibid., p. 489.
[19] Bancroft, II, 436.
[20] Latané, A Hist. of Amer. For. Pol., p. 412; also, Schofield's
Forty-Six Years in the Army, p. 385.
[21] Ibid., pp. 222-228, for more detailed account.

It has been the President's purpose that France should be respectfully informed upon two points; namely, first, that the United States earnestly desire to continue and to cultivate sincere friendship with France. Second, that this policy would be brought into imminent jeopardy unless France could deem it consistent with her interests and honor to desist from the prosecution of armed intervention in Mexico, to overthrow the domestic republican government existing there, and to establish upon its ruins the foreign monarchy which has been attempted to be inaugurated in the capital of the country.[22]

Apparently this was a command to withdraw or fight.

Early in January of 1866, Drouyn de Lhuys reviewed the course that France had followed, and as a condition of withdrawal of French troops, he again attempted to get the United States to recognize Maximilian.[23] On February 12, Seward replied that the proceedings in Mexico were regarded in the United States as having been taken without the authority and prosecuted against the opinion and will of the Mexican people; that the United States had not seen any satisfactory evidence which would lead her to believe that the people of Mexico had spoken, and had called into being or accepted the so-called empire which had been established at the capital. He emphasized the withdrawal of the French forces in order that such proceedings be permitted to take their course. To quote:

Of course, the Emperor of France is entitled to determine the aspect in which the Mexican situation ought to be regarded by him. Nevertheless, the view which I have thus presented is the one which this nation has accepted. It, therefore, recognizes and must continue to recognize in Mexico only the ancient republic. and it can in no case consent to involve itself, either directly or indirectly, in relations with or recognition of the institution of the Prince Maximilian in Mexico.[24]

He concluded:

We shall be gratified when the Emperor shall give to us definite information of the time when French military operations may be expected to cease in Mexico.[25]

Napoleon decided that he could not afford to risk a war with the United States. On April 5, 1866, " Le Moniteur "

---

[22] Dip. Cor., 1865-1866, Part III, 491, Mr. Seward to Mr. Bigelow, December 16, 1865.   [24] Ibid., p. 815.
[23] Ibid., pp. 805-808.   [25] Ibid., p. 820.

announced that the Emperor had decided to withdraw French troops from Mexico in three detachments; the first to leave in November, 1866, the second in March, 1867, and the third in November, 1867.[26] Thus the question of French intervention in Mexico appeared to be settled.

When the time came for the departure of the first third of the French army, Mr. Seward was informed by Mr. Bigelow, American Minister in Paris, that Napoleon had decided to postpone the withdrawal until the spring of 1867.[27] Seward replied on November 23, 1866:

We cannot acquiesce—
First, because the term 'next Spring' as appointed for the entire evacuation is indefinite and vague.
Second, because we have no authority for stating to Congress and to the American people that we have now a better guarantee for the withdrawal of the whole expeditionary force in the Spring than we have heretofore had for the withdrawal of a part in November.[28]

A third reason was given which in effect was that such delay would seriously conflict with the plans of the United States and would lead greatly to her embarrassment.[29]

No doubt Napoleon had intended to withdraw his troops. The reason for delaying the act was to protect as long as possible French securities and in a way to redeem himself for the part he had played in the attempt to establish Maximilian. While stalling for time, he proposed that a provisional government be established in Mexico in which neither Juarez nor Maximilian would have a share. Mr. Seward refused to act, but continued to recognize the Juarez government as the only legitimate rule in Mexico.[30] The northeastern part of Mexico again fell under the control of the republican gov-

---

[26] Ibid., p. 827.
[27] Ibid., 1866-1867, Part I, 364.
[28] Ibid., p. 366.
[29] Ibid., p. 367.
[30] Ibid., 1862-1863, I, 748. As early as 1862, the United States signed a treaty agreeing to furnish Juarez with money and munitions in order that the war against Maximilian might be continued. In the early part of 1866, General Sheridan supplied as many as thirty thousand muskets.

ernment,[31] and thus Seward, believing his position entirely safe, declined Napoleon's proposition on January 18, 1867.[32] Napoleon now gave up all hope of establishing an empire in North America.

In February, 1867, the French evacuated Mexico City.[33] Apparently in accordance with the wishes of the United States government, the empire ended, giving way to Juarez and his cabinet, who re-entered the Capital and established anew the Republic. Whether the affair can be hailed as a triumph of the Monroe Doctrine, or as a result of conditions of internal European politics at the time is not a question that we need answer here. The fact which most interested the United States was that intervention came to an end.

One of the most interesting features about the story just narrated is the way in which Mr. Seward handled the whole matter. As we have seen, France violated the Monroe Doctrine for a period of five years. Quite naturally one would expect to find Seward's despatches frequently referring to " colonization," " political system," " Monroe Doctrine," and the like. But such is not the case. Nowhere do we find these terms mentioned; nor is precedent called into use. He declared from the beginning that it was the policy of the United States " to leave the destinies of Mexico in the keeping of her own people."

In 1867, Seward advanced to the point of demanding withdrawal upon the grounds that the American peoples had a right to choose their own form of government. And again, he deeply resented the hostility shown his country by France in attempting to establish a despotic government to the south of her.

It seems that facts will support these statements: neither Lincoln nor Johnson gave much thought or time to Mexico during this period, while upon Seward the burden of handling the diplomacy of the situation appears to have rested. But be it remembered that his acts as concerned the entire

[31] Memoirs of Gen. W. T. Sherman, II, 224.
[32] Dip. Cor., 1867, I, 218.
[33] Ibid., II, 356.

5

matter were always in accordance with the will and desires of the administration and that of the Union.

The United States had witnessed, beginning with Iturbide in 1823, the rise and fall of thirty-six different governments in Mexico, extending over a period of almost forty years.[34] To each new government she accorded recognition with little delay or hesitation, but from the very beginning she turned a deaf ear to Maximilian and his attempted empire. Mexico was to be given an opportunity to solve her own problem free from European intervention.

---

[34] See Appendix.

CHAPTER V

THE DIAZ GOVERNMENT

Only once in a period extending from 1859 until 1911 was the United States forced to consider the question of according recognition to a Mexican government. We have seen that recognition was refused to Emperor Maximilian while President Juarez was regarded as being the true head of the Mexican government throughout the period. This recognition thus accorded to the federal and constitutional government was continued without interruption until the death of Juarez in 1872, and even after that through the administration of his successor, Lerdo de Tejada.[1]

In 1872, an unsuccessful insurrection broke out headed by General Porfirio Diaz, who claimed that he had been defeated for the presidency by fraud. We mention this fact to show the basis of the revolutionary plan. Diaz's claim was then to reestablish free suffrage and honesty in the holding of elections. In this first attempt, as has been noted, he met with failure, but in 1875 a revolution was started anew in which Diaz won over both Lerdo de Tejada and Iglesias. An order was issued for a new and free election in which the country voted almost unanimously for Diaz.[2] As a result, he called in March of 1877 a Congress consisting of two hundred and thirty-seven members, and constitutional order was entirely restored.[3] The United States formally accorded recognition to the Diaz government in May 1878,[4] after which constitutional presidential succession was the rule in Mexico until the overthrow of Diaz by Madero.

It was believed that upon the fall of President Tejada

---

[1] For a more detailed account, read the introduction of Mr. John W. Foster's remarks before the subcommittee of the committee on foreign affairs to investigate the Mexican question. Despatches from Mexico, LXI.

[2] John W. Foster, Memoirs, I, 87.

[3] Despatches from Mexico, LXI, Foster's remarks before the subcommittee on foreign affairs.

[4] Moore, I, 148.

the independent movements would unite by the recognition of Iglesias as provisional President and General Diaz as the Minister of War and Commander of the Army. Such appeared to be the desire of the country and of those most experienced with the administration of the government. On the other hand, Diaz's revolutionary friends and those who had fought his battles demanded that he become head of the government, and he yielded.[5]

Before the February elections in 1877, Diaz made no formal request for the recognition of his government by the United States, although it is true that he confidently expected it, if the elections were favorable to him. This view was later admitted by Señor Vallarta, his Minister of Foreign Relations.[6] Diaz's confidence seems to have been based to a great extent upon his stand with respect to the findings of the Mixed Claims Commission. This was a joint commission which, since July 4, 1868, had been adjudicating claims between the United States and Mexico that had arisen since the Treaty of Guadalupe Hidalgo in 1848. This Commission reported on December 14, 1876, a net balance of about four millions in favor of the United States.[7] This sum Mexico was obligated to pay to the United States in annual installments of $300,000, the first of which fell due on January 31, 1877.[8] Although the formal report was not made until December 14, 1876, its main provisions must have been known earlier, for when Diaz became provisional President he announced his intention to pay the United States the first installment of $300,000 when it was due in January of 1877. Mr. Foster at once reported this to his government at Washington as an indication of the intentions of Diaz to meet the obligations of past governments.[9]

---

[5] 45th Cong., 2d sess., Ex. Doc. No. I, Mr. Foster to Mr. Fish, November 28, 1876.
[6] 45th Cong., 2d sess., H. Ex. Doc. No. I, 410, Mr. Foster to Mr. Evart, June 20, 1877.
[7] H. H. Bancroft, History of Mexico, p. 443.
[8] 45th Cong., 2d sess., H. Ex. Doc. No. I, 388, Mr. Fish to Mr. Foster, December 20, 1876.
[9] Ibid., p. 385. Mr. Foster, December 20, 1876. In Despatch No.

Though Diaz was apparently quite willing to await the outcome of the February elections before asking recognition from the United States, it is rather interesting to note that the Grant administration, embarrassed at the prospect of not being able to collect the $300,000 installment of an indemnity from an unrecognized government, gave Mr. Foster discretionary authority to recognize the Diaz provisional government.[10]

When the Mixed Claims Commission made its report, on December 14, 1876, it also filed a joint expense account which gave to Mexico a balance of more than $57,000.[11] Four days after the filing of this report, Secretary of State Fish instructed Mr. Foster to ascertain whether Mexico desired to deduct the whole of this $57,000 from the first installment of the $300,000 or to distribute it throughout the period of payment.[12]

Mr. Fish instructed Mr. Foster on January 19, 1877, that word had reached Washington of the defeat of all forces arrayed against Porfirio Diaz and that the latter might be regarded as the actual ruler of the country. He continued:

Inasmuch, therefore, as we cannot receive from a government which we do not acknowledge the installment of indemnity payable by Mexico on the 31st instant, on this account especially you would be warranted in recognizing the government of Profirio Diaz, unless, before this reaches you such a step should be made inexpedient by events which are not now foreseen. You will exercise your best discretion in the matter. From our point of view, we cannot comprehend the expediency on the part of Diaz of disowning the official contracts entered into by his predecessor . . . you will express the regret which we should have at the effect of the measure upon those

487, January 16, 1877, Mr. Foster writes to Mr. Fish in part, as follows:

". . . While I was as yet without instructions from you on the subject, I did not think you would recognize the principle that one government of Mexico had the power to disannul the legal contracts and solemn engagements entered into by the preceding government with citizens of the United States, while that government was recognized by the United States and other nations as the legitimate and constitutional government of Mexico. . . ."

[10] Instructions to Ministers, Mexico, XIX, 317-319, Mr. Fish to Mr. Foster, January 19, 1877.

[11] 45th Cong., 2d sess., H. Ex. Doc. No. I, 389, Mr. Foster to Mr. Fish, November 28, 1876.

[12] Ibid., p. 388.

interests of citizens of the United States who may have entered into contracts with the Lerdo government. If, however, the policy avowed should be insisted upon and carried into execution it is not expected that, for the present at least, you will regard this as an international question.[13]

Judging from the statement just cited, it seems apparent that Mr. Fish held the repudiation by Diaz of the claims of Americans made under the preceding governments as of secondary consideration as compared with the collection of the first installment of the indemnity and the recognition of the government by our own.

Before the above quoted instructions reached Mr. Foster, the latter was informed by Señor Vallarta, who was at that time Minister of Foreign Relations in the Diaz Cabinet, that the $300,000 covering the first installment of the Mexican indemnity had already been sent to Vera Cruz for shipment to the United States, and that Mexico would take the permitted deduction of $57,000 in making her first payment.[14] Mr. Foster on his own initiative made this communication the basis for an expression of the agreement between himself and Señor Vallarta. He wrote on June 20, 1877, to Secretary Evarts:

The receipt by Mr. Fish of the first installment of the claims award could not be cited as any indication of the intention of my government to recognize that of General Diaz, as Mr. Vallarta would remember that it was expressly understood between us before the commissioner left Mexico to make the payment, that its receipt was not to involve the question of recognition in any manner. The records of the Mexican foreign office will show that the present policy of my government as to the frontier is the same as that assumed or foreshadowed during all my residence in Mexico. . . .[15]

Later, when writing unofficially, Mr. Foster commented upon this incident in the following manner:

The acceptance of this payment from the Diaz Government would constitute a recognition of it on the part of the United States, and the policy of the latter was not to be hasty in recognizing a revolutionary party established on the overthrow of the constitutional government. I was authorized, however, by Secretary Fish to make

---

[13] Instructions to Ministers, Mexico, XIX, 317-319.
[14] Ibid., p. 321.
[15] Despatches from Ministers, Mexico, Mr. Foster to Mr. Evarts, June 20, 1877.

the recognition, if it became necessary, in order to enable Mexico to comply with the treaty and make the payment. But the Diaz government, realizing this situation, agreed to make the payment through Señor Mariscal, the Mexican Minister in Washington, accredited by the Lerdo Administration, and through the accommodating spirit of the Diaz government that question was for the occasion avoided.[16]

Very soon after the collection of the first installment of the Mexican indemnity the Grant Administration passed out of power on March 4, 1877, and left to the incoming Hayes régime the burden of dealing with Mexico and her problems.

There is little doubt but that General Diaz was head of a " de facto " government, and heretofore such a ruler had been accorded almost immediate recognition by the United States. Not so in this case. Early in March of 1877, Mr. Foster said that he had made no formal or written declaration of recognition of the Diaz Government, but had simply entered into an unofficial relationship with it as the " de facto " and only existing government in the country.[17]

The strength and power of General Diaz increased so rapidly that Mr. Foster wrote to Secretary Fish on January 19, 1877, saying:

Both Mr. Lerdo and Mr. Iglesias have left Mexican territory; so that there is no rival claimant to General Diaz in the Republic, and virtually the whole country has submitted to his authority. The only opposition known to exist is by Governor Alvarez with a small part of the state of Guerrero, and our consul at Acapulco informs me that Alvarez is ready to surrender his authority to General Diaz and is only resisting the opposing Governor.[18]

One month later, just after the February election, Mr. Foster related that the election had been favorable to Diaz and " that steps were at once taken to have the revolutionary government assume the character of a constitutional one." [19] Mr. Foster also mentioned the fact that General Diaz had more than met requirements as laid down by the traditional

---

[16] Foster, Diplomatic Memoirs, I, 87.
[17] Despatches, Mexico, No. 502, Mr. Foster to Mr. Fish, March 3, 1877.
[18] Ibid., Despatch No. 496, Mr. Foster to Mr. Fish, January 19, 1877.
[19] Foster, Diplomatic Memoirs, I, 87.

policy of the United States for recognition;[20] that he had not only fulfilled international obligations, but had also promised to give attention to the preservation of order on the frontier and the prevention of raids into Texas from the Mexican side of the Rio Grande.[21] Apparently Mr. Foster believed it time to take the final step, but did not feel that his instructions warranted it.

Prior to February 1877, no direct move had been made on the part of Diaz to secure recognition by the United States, but after he had been elected to office by an overwhelming majority and the constitutional order had been restored he became anxious as to the action of his northern neighbor. Soon after the election Mr. Vallarta transmitted a note to the Secretary of State, and with it a sealed letter from General Diaz to the President of the United States, in which it was called to the attention of the latter that the votes of the electors had been cast almost unanimously for General Diaz, and that his election by Congress would be a mere formality. This letter was not answered, for the President deemed it advisable to await the proceedings of the Mexican Congress.[22]

As has been remarked, the traditional policy of the United States had been only to require as a prerequisite to recognition the establishment of an effective " de facto " government, but Hayes refused to allow precedent to dictate his course.[23] Mexico's failure to handle satisfactorily the border situation at this time became involved with the problem of recognition. It will be recalled that for years prior to 1877, there had been repeated appeals coming from the Rio Grande border because of the injuries and raids brought about by the Indians of Mexico.[24]

Secretary of State Evarts in his instructions to Foster on March 31, 1877, wrote:

---

[20] 45th Cong., 1st and 2d sess., H. Reports, Doc. No. 701, p. 38.
[21] Despatches, Mexico, No. 503, Mr. Foster to Mr. Fish, March 3, 1877.
[22] Ibid., Despatch No. 504, Mr. Foster to Sec. Fish, March 4, 1877.
[23] Richardson, Messages and Papers of the Presidents. See Hayes First Annual Message, December 3, 1877, VI, 468.
[24] 45th Cong., 1st sess., H. Ex. Doc. No. 13, p. 5.

As the authorities seem to be unable and unwilling to check the depredations, the President may soon have to take into serious consideration the expediency of acting pursuant to Colonel Shafter's opinion. Undoubtly it would be preferable to enter Mexican territory for the purpose indicated with consent or with the acquiescence of the government of that Republic. If, however, these should be refused and the outrages persisted in, this government may deem itself warranted in punishing the wrong-doers wherever they may be found.[25]

Soon after receiving the above instructions, Mr. Foster entered into a full discussion of the entire matter with Señor Vallarta. In this conference Señor Vallarta was reminded of the fact that the Diaz government from its beginning had been impressed with the importance of maintaining peace and order on the frontier, and that such was necessary to the maintenance of peace and friendly relations between the two countries.[26] It was also recalled that Mexico had failed to comply with these wishes, much to the displeasure of the United States.[27] Señor Vallarta readily agreed that in order to maintain peace successfully on the frontier it would be necessary for the military forces on both sides of the Rio Grande to cooperate, but he hastened to add "in order to make this cooperation fully effective it was highly desirable first to have the official relations between the two governments restored." [28] Mr. Foster's reply was that the peace on the frontier should not be endangered because of a delay in the formal recognition by the United States.[29]

On May 15, 1877, a report of Mr. Foster's conference with Señor Vallarta reached Washington.[30] The next day Mr. Evarts instructed our representative at Mexico City, as regarded recognition, in the following manner:

The government of the United States in its dealing with the Mexican Republic has aimed to pursue not merely a just but a generous and friendly course. While earnest to guard and protect the rights of its own citizens and the safety of its own territory, it does not seek to intervene in political contents or changes of administration. It is accustomed to accept and recognize the result of a popular choice in Mexico, and not to scrutinize closely the regularity or

---

[25] Ibid., p. 4. Mr. Evarts to Mr. Foster, March 31, 1877.
[26] For. Rel., 1877, p. 401, Mr. Foster to Mr. Evarts, April 24, 1877.
[27] Ibid., p. 402. [29] Ibid.
[28] Ibid. [30] Ibid., p. 401.

irregularity of the methods by which Presidents are inaugurated. In the present case it waits before recognizing General Diaz as the President of Mexico until it shall be assured that his election is approved by the Mexican people, and that his administration is possessed of stability to endure and of disposition to comply with the rules of international comity and obligations of treaties.

Such recognition, if accorded, would imply something more than a mere formal assent. It would imply a belief that the government so recognized will faithfully execute its duties and observe the spirit of its treaties. The recognition of a President in Mexico by the United States has an important moral influence, which, as you explain, is appreciated at the capitol of that Republic. . . . You justly remark that in fifty years there have been about sixty changes of administration in Mexico, and it may be added that those administrations have been longest lived that were most faithful and friendly in the discharge of their treaty obligations to the United States.

When the recent revolution resulted in placing General Diaz in the position of Chief Magistrate, this government learned with satisfaction that he was desirous that the 4th of July, 1868, between the two countries should be faithfully observed and that he had accordingly sanctioned the prompt payment of the installment of two hundred and fifty thousand and five hundred and one dollars in gold.[31]

After calling attention to the numerous injuries suffered by American citizens in their lives and property rights, and urging that Mexico make some compensation for these infringements, Mr. Evarts continued:

It is not difficult to believe that General Diaz and his Minister of Foreign Affairs earnestly desire friendly relations and recognition on the part of the United States, and it is gratifying to receive the assurances unofficially made through you that they are disposed to adjust and rectify these complaints and grievances, and are not unwilling to consent to some arrangement for concerted action between the military commanders of the two countries on the frontier, for the preservation of peace and order and the protection of life and property. It is natural that Mexican statesmen should urge upon you the argument that the restoration of official relations between the two governments would open the way towards such an adjustment. But it is natural, on the other hand, that the government of the United States should be disposed to believe that some guarantee of such an arrangement should be made the condition precedent to any recognition, rather than to trust to the possibility that it may ultimately follow.[32]

Such a forceful expression of policy only served to remove recognition further and further into the background, and at

---

[31] Instructions from the State Department, Mexico, XIX, Doc. No 390, pp. 336-340. Mr. Evarts to Mr. Foster, May 16, 1877.
[32] Ibid., p. 339.

times it appeared as if the two countries would be brought
into war over the maintenance of order upon the frontier.[33]
In such a condition were the relations between the United
States and Mexico when in June of 1877, Señor Vallarta and
Mr. Foster met in another conference. Here Señor Vallarta
contended that:

The government of General Diaz possessed all the conditions of
recognition required by international law and the practice of nations,
and as a proof of this cited the fact that the European powers represented in Mexico as well as Central American republics had already
recognized the present government, leaving the United States in a
singular and independent position, which she sought to explain by
the unfriendly attitude of the administration of President Hayes.
He claimed that the present government of Mexico had manifested
every possible disposition to comply with the obligations of treaty
and comity towards the United States; that it had promptly paid
the first installment on the Mexico claim awards under the most
difficult circumstances; and that it had held itself ready to give all
reasonable guarantees for the preservation of peace on the frontier
and for the protection of American interests in Mexico; but as he
[Mr. Vallarta] had stated to me on other occasions, the adjustment
of these questions would properly follow recognition, especially
where they required treaty stipulations.[34]

Mr. Foster was quick to remind Señor Vallarta that every
nation was free to decide for itself the time and manner of
recognizing a new and revolutionary government.[35] He remarked that the United States was interested in, and desired
to familiarize herself with the incoming government's ability
and disposition to comply with its international obligations
both on the frontier and towards American citizens and
interests within the country.[36] When Señor Vallarta accused
the Hayes administration of a change in policy from that of
the preceding régime, Mr. Foster replied:

. . . If the government of General Diaz has not up to the present
time been recognized by that of the United States, it is owing to its
own neglect of plain duties. Mr. Vallarta will remember that six
months ago, soon after entering the Foreign Office, I called his atten-

---

[33] For a detailed account see 45th Cong., 1st sess., H. Ex. Doc.
No. 13, pp. 12-18; also 45th Cong., 1st and 2d sess., H. Reports,
Doc. No. 701, p. 240; For. Rel., 1877-1878, I, 411-418.
[34] For. Rel., 1877, p. 410, Mr. Foster to Mr. Evarts, June 20, 1877.
[35] Despatches, Mexico, Mr. Foster to Mr. Evarts, June 20, 1877.
[36] Ibid.

tion to the critical condition of affairs on the Rio Grande frontier and stated that they more seriously threatened the peace of the two countries than any and all other matters. I referred to the raids in Texas by Mexican bandits, the ravages of the Indians, and the annoyances of the *Zons Libre*. There has been no change of policy on the part of the government of the United States with the change of administration as he [Mr. Vallarta] inconsiderately asserted.[37]

Later in his Diplomatic Memoirs, Mr. Foster admitted that Señor Vallarta no doubt was right when he intimated that a change in administration had produced a change in the policy of the United States. To quote:

There is no doubt of the correctness of his [Señor Vallarta's] statement that there had been a change of policy as to recognition after the inauguration of President Hayes, and there was some foundation for this change that a scheme had been formed to bring on a war through the Texas troubles.[38]

If we are to judge solely from Mr. Evarts' instructions, it appears that our State Department became more stringent in its demands upon Mexico. On August 2, 1877, Mr. Foster was instructed that any stipulations in regard to treaty between the two countries

. . . must deal explicitly and clearly with the question of the use of military force to pursue offenders and recapture stolen property, even beyond the territorial limits of the United States if no other way can be found for checking such depredations.

It is deemed preferable, however, that the conference upon these points, must necessarily precede any recognition of General Diaz. . . . You are instructed, therefore, to continue your unofficial intercourse with Mr. Vallarta and to report from time to time as you ascertain them precisely what definite terms the government of General Diaz would be willing, and would deem itself able to accede to. You will enter fully into discussion of the various subjects, the border raids, the action of military commanders, the question of forced loans. . . . Meanwhile the government of the United States will reserve its decision upon the question of recognizing the government of General Diaz to await such information as it may receive from you.[39]

It has been noted that the Hayes administration in its earliest days demanded cooperation of Mexico in the effective

---

[37] Ibid.
[38] Foster, I, 92.
[39] Instructions to Ministers, Mexico, XIX, 356, Mr. Evarts to Mr. Foster, August 2, 1877.

suppression of border raids and disturbances. Now Secretary Evarts took a more advanced step: he demanded that Mexico give the United States the right of pursuing offenders across the border, and that such was a necessary prerequisite to a treaty covering all disputes between the two countries. The United States held the signing of such a treaty a prerequisite to recognition. For the first time in her relations with Mexico the United States demanded the signing of a treaty prior to the granting of recognition.

Carrying out the instructions of the Secretary of State, Mr. Foster sought other conferences with Vallarta. In his report to Mr. Evarts on September 4, 1877, he characterized this interview in the following manner:

> It will be seen that the Mexican Government has resisted step by step the proposition for a reciprocal crossing of troops in pursuit of raiders; and at last it has not consented to it, although I infer from Mr. Vallarta's declaration at our last conference that his government will eventually agree to it. As I considered this measure a *sine qua non* to the arrangement of a treaty, I deemed it unnecessary to enter minutely into an examination of the articles of the . . . project or of the other necessary details, until we had first settled satisfactorily that essential measure.[40]

Again, on November 8, 1877, Mr. Foster said that it had been made apparent that the Diaz government was not disposed to adjust the question of forced loans either by a treaty stipulation, by the enactment of a federal law, or by the recognition and payment of the forced loans levied by its own leaders during the recent revolution; that such claims held by foreigners as the existing government might recognize as binding upon it would be treated as a part of the domestic debt of Mexico. He remarked that Señor Vallarta still declined to grant permission for the reciprocal crossing of troops, which the United States continued to insist upon as being an essential measure to be inserted in a treaty between the two countries. Also Señor Vallarta had failed to give any information concerning the numerous disputes which

---

[40] 45th Cong., 2d sess., Reports of Committees, 1877-78, Appendix G, p. 454.

arose in the July conferences and which he had promised to settle at an early date.[41]

President Hayes in his first annual message on December 3, 1877, expressed the policy of the administration as follows:

It has been the custom of the United States, when such changes of government have heretofore occurred in Mexico, to recognize and enter into official relations with the " de facto " government as soon as it should appear to have the approval of the Mexican people and should manifest a disposition to adhere to the obligations of treaties and international friendship. In the present case such official recognition has been deferred by the occurrences on the Rio Grande border, the records of which have been already communicated to each House of Congress in answer to their respective resolutions of inquiry. . . . The best interests of both countries required the maintenance of peace upon the border and the development of commerce between the two Republics. . . . I yet must ask the attention of Congress to the actual occurrences on the border, that the lives and property of our citizens may be adequately protected and peace preserved.[42]

If we are to judge from President Hayes' own words, the year of 1877 closed with the two republics apparently further divided over the much disputed question than had heretofore been the case.

It is noteworthy to remark here that both houses of the United States Congress in the latter part of 1877, and early in the following year, gave the Mexican situation more than a passing notice.[43] But neither the Committee on Foreign Affairs in the House nor the special Committee appointed by the Senate to investigate " border conditions " made any formal report until after Hayes had reversed his policy in regard to Mexico.[44] As a result of the interest manifested by Congress with regard to this matter, Mr. Foster was called to Washington to make a report before the Subcommittee of the Committee on Foreign Affairs to investigate the Mexican question.[45] Mr. Schleicher, the chairman of the committee, asked the following question of Mr. Foster:

---

[41] Ibid., pp. 456, 457.
[42] Richardson, VII, 468.
[43] For detailed account see 45th Cong., 1st sess., H. Ex. Doc. No. 13, p. 1; 45th Cong., 2d sess., H. J., p. 163; 45th Cong., 1st and 2d sess., H. Reports Doc. No. 701, p. 38.
[44] Ibid.
[45] Despatches from Mexico, February 16, 1878, LXI.

Question—We would be glad to have an expression of your views upon the subject of our commercial relations with Mexico. How are they affected by the delay in recognizing the government of Diaz, and also by what means they could be furthered in the future?

Answer—The delay in recognition has had a tendency to irritate the Mexican people and they interpret it as an unfriendly act towards them. That does not have a tendency to build up commerce very much in itself. One of the great obstacles to developing our commercial relations with Mexico is the insecurity to property and capital in the country. Capital is more sensitive to protection than even life. People will risk their lives where they would not their money. The unsettled condition of the country is a great impediment in the way of increasing our commercial relations by American investments in Mexico. It ought not, however, to entirely prevent it. If we had railroad communication, we would have a great advantage over European nations. . . .

In speaking of protection of American capital invested in Mexico, Mr. Foster made the statement that the country to the south of the Rio Grande was always willing to promise more than she could fulfil. As concerns recognition, he continued:

Our interest is for free government. That once established it should show its stability and its strength, and the trouble in Mexico is that reproach is brought upon free government by the ease and frequency of their revolutionary changes. I cannot, therefore, think that it is the good part of a republic like ours to encourage by the rapidity of our recognition the rapidity of their changes; and if I were to express an opinion as to the effect of. non-recognition thus far upon the Mexican administration at home it would be this, that it has really given more actual stability to Diaz than if recognition had been made, and produced more actual and serious efforts on the part of Mexico to practically discharge its duties to this country on the frontier.

Now I have no hesitation in saying that Mexico, all things being considered, has shown a considerable disposition to discharge its duties as a border state towards us, and that when the congressional investigation shall have resulted in a presentation of their view of the facts and the course of things it will be a matter for the government to decide very promptly whether we shall adopt the plan of recognition and then a pretty earnest demand for satisfactory assurances or whether we shall . . . require some understanding about the treaty stipulations before recognition. The real difficulty between us and Mexico is that while it stands as a civilized power with all the pride and self opinion that belongs to a strong civilized nation, it has not the power to carry out towards us the obligations which such a condition imparts, and that will be a trouble that cannot be removed by the formalities of negotiation. . . . [46]

---

[46] Despatches from Mexico, LXI, Mr. Foster's report before the subcommittee of the Committee on Foreign Affairs, February 16, 1878.

In the course of the report, Mr. Foster mentioned the fact that General Diaz had shown more energy in the preservation of order on the frontier than had previous Mexican Governments; that the country was ruled in peace and in accordance with the Constitution; that Diaz was apparently all-powerful and in all likelihood would remain in power for some time. When asked what he thought ought to be the action of the government in reference to the recognition of the Diaz government, Mr. Foster replied that he believed that was a question for the Secretary of State to answer. Whereupon with the acquiescence of the entire committee, the question was withdrawn as one not proper to be answered by Mr. Foster.[47]

After having Mr. Foster's report, it appears that the President and Secretary Evarts concluded it better not to delay recognition further, for Foster returned to Mexico in an official capacity.[48] Secretary Evarts justified his reversal of policy as set forth in May of 1877, upon this ground:

It is now several months since you were informed by the Department that the government of the United States before recognizing General Diaz as the President of Mexico waited to be assured that his administration was approved by the Mexican people, and was possessed of due stability and animated by a disposition to comply with the rules of international comity and the obligations of treaties.

The information which you have communicated since that date in your successive despatches in reference to the internal affairs of Mexico, seems to show that General Diaz has been able to preserve peace for the most part in the country, and that his authority continues to be recognized practically throughout the entire republic.

As regards the disposition to comply with obligations of treaties, it has been gratifying to the government of the United States to observe on the part of the present authorities of Mexico an increased desire to preserve peace and good order on the frontier and an endeavor to adopt more vigorous and efficient measures to repress border depredations and raids on the territory of the United States. The prompt payment of two successive installments of the award of the American Mexican Claims Commission is also accepted by this government as a substantial evidence of a disposition to observe treaty stipulations.

You state, however, that the government of General Diaz finds itself embarrassed in the discussion of pending matters of difference between the two nations, and placed under constraint in reaching a satisfactory settlement of those matters by the absence of recogni-

---

[47] Ibid.
[48] Ibid., XIX, 397-399. Mr. Evarts to Mr. Foster, March 23, 1878.

tion on the part of the government of the United States. If this view of the situation be honestly entertained by the government of General Diaz, it is better for this government to waive its own preferences as to the fittest manner and time of adjusting the difficulties, sufficiently grave, which have prevented a good understanding with a sister republic, with which we have so many interests in common. The President animated by an earnest desire to remove every impediment to an adjustment of all disputed questions between the two governments will, therefore, authorize you to inform Mr. Vallarta that he deems it no longer necessary or desirable to defer the resumption of diplomatic relations and the official recognition of the authorities with whom you have so long held unofficial intercourse. You are authorized to say to Mr. Vallarta that henceforth your communications will be official and in the usual form with recognized powers.[49]

In a formal note to Señor Vallarta, dated April 9, 1878, Mr. Foster expressed both the gratification of the United States government and his own personal satisfaction at the resumption of official relations between the two countries. The next day Señor Vallarta replied to Mr. Foster saying that the Mexican republic joined with him in expressing like sentiments towards the United States.[50]

Thus, by the interchange of notes, formal recognition was granted the Diaz government by the United States. This recognition was not interrupted for a period of twenty-seven years. During these years the country underwent a period of outward stability but internal oppression. General Diaz maintained his power by military might. He almost entirely suppressed banditry; he encouraged foreign capital to enter the country; some progress was made along educational lines, but his illegal appropriation of the land created a situation which caused his downfall and made for international difficulties.

From what has been said it seems clear that recognition of the Diaz Government was apparently based upon three factors: (1) "de facto" control by the new revolutionary government; (2) apparent popular approval of the new government; (3) the disposition of the new government to adhere to the obligation of treaties and international friendship. The last of these factors was a new test for recognition.

---

[49] Ibid.
[50] Ibid., Enclosure No. I, in Doc. No. 689, Mr. Foster to Mr. Vallarta, April 9, 1878.

6

CHAPTER VI

RECOGNITION SINCE 1910

Diaz's dictatorship was brought to an end through propaganda promoted by Francisco Madero, a member of an influential family in Northern Mexico, who had received most of his education in the United States. In the fall of 1910, he presented himself as a candidate for the Presidency against Diaz, but instead of being elected he found a prison cell. After his release, he continued his propaganda from the safer soil of the United States. The northern provinces found much that they liked in Madero's promises, for they had suffered long from the exploitation of their natural resources by foreigners and the acquisition of vast estates by a few.[1]

Many people believe another cause of the Madero Revolution was the secret support of the American Government. Many Mexicans held that our interest was intrusive and that our policy was affected by Diaz's effort to play British against American oil interests in such manner as to prevent the influence of the United States from becoming predominant. Diaz's nationalization of the railroads served as an additional check upon American strength in Mexico.

The insurrection spread like wild fire and the government of Diaz soon fell apart. On May 7, 1911, he professed his willingness to retire, " after peace was restored." Eighteen days later he decided to resign without further delay. He left the country at once, and Francisco de la Barra became Provisional President pending an election.[2]

When Secretary Knox became aware that de la Barra had assumed control of the Government, he was quick to express confidence in his power and best wishes for a successful administration.[3]

---

[1] Herbert I. Priestly, International Relations Pamphlets, I, 5-6.
[2] For. Rel., 1911, No. 1465, Mr. Zamalona to Mr. Knox, May 27, 1911.
[3] Ibid., p. 353. Mr. Knox to de la Barra.

On October 1, 1911, the people of Mexico participated in their first general election of a really popular kind.[4] There was only slight opposition to the candidacy of Madero, leader of the revolution, and his running mate for the Vice-Presidency, Piño Suarez. They were duly chosen and inaugurated.[5] Mr. Henry Lane Wilson, speaking of his election, said:

It may be said that the elections, while free from the influences of official menace through the police and army, were nevertheless farcical in character and in a very small degree representative of Mexican public opinion.[6]

According to Wilson, disorder continued in a large part of the country and crimes of all sorts were committed within forty miles of the capital city.[7]

Despite the view of our minister, that Madero's election was "farcical in character and in a very small degree representative of Mexican public opinion," the United States entered into regular relations with the new government and even went so far as to suppress revolutionary movements from the United States directed against it.[8] Perhaps sympathy with the movement which Madero headed had some effect upon the rapidity with which the Department of State acted.

In February 1913, President Taft wrote to President Madero in the following manner:

In view of the special friendship and relations between the two countries, I cannot too strongly impress upon Your Excellency the vital importance of the early establishment of that real peace and order which this Government has so long hoped to see, both because American citizens and their property must be protected and respected and also because this nation sympathizes deeply with the afflictions of the Mexican people.[9]

---

[4] Ibid., September 4, 1911, Despatch 887.
[5] Ibid., October 18, 1911, Despatch 1034, Wilson to Knox; also, ibid., November 6, 1911 (telegram), Wilson to Knox.
[6] Ibid., 1911, p. 519.
[7] Ibid., 1911, Despatch 1934, Wilson to Knox, October 18, 1911. Mr. Wilson speaking later of the Madero government said that it was anti-American in its attitude and even more despotic than the rule of General Diaz (For. Rel., February 26, 1917, p. 741, Wilson to Knox, telegram).
[8] Ibid., 1911, pp. 520-525.
[9] Ibid., p. 715. Taft to Madero, February 16, 1913.

He mentioned the fact that during the past two years the course of events had culminated in a dangerous situation, and that much pessimism was aroused in the United States. He urged that it was of paramount importance for Mexico to relieve this situation promptly.

Like many others, Madero found it easier to arouse the storm of popular discontent than to remedy the evils. He seemed rather devoid of either political judgment or executive ability. Consequently, discontent grew up in all quarters, and on February 9, 1913, a conspiracy headed by Victoriano Huerta, Felix Diaz, and Bernardo Reyes culminated in an open attack upon the National Palace.[10] After ten days of anarchy in the capital city, Madero finally surrendered, resigned his office under pressure, and with his Vice-President was assassinated on the following night, under circumstances which created a strong presumption that General Huerta had a hand in the deed.[11]

The army at once proclaimed General Huerta Provisional President, and the choice was immediately ratified by a subservient Congress. From the very beginning it was evident that General Huerta would be unable to establish order. He was purely a military ruler, and by support of the army he remained in office for seventeen months. Two farcical elections were held during this period, but no one dared become a candidate in opposition to Huerta. He assumed dictatorial power until overthrown by Carranza.

As early as February 21, 1913, Henry Lane Wilson urged the Taft administration to grant recognition to the Huerta government in order that the new government be enabled to

---

[10] Ibid., pp. 699-701, Wilson to Knox, February 9, 1913.

[11] Ibid., p. 723, Wilson to Knox, February 19, 1913.

[12] Ibid., 1913, p. 741. The same view was expressed a little later in a communication to Secretary Bryan, which reads in part, as follows: " I must again urge upon the President that on the highest grounds of policy—which in this case I understand to be the conserving and the extension of our material interests in Mexico, the restoration of peace, and the cultivation of sentiments of friendship and respect with a neighboring and friendly nation—we should, without further delay, following the example of all governments

impose its authority and reestablish order.[12] But President Taft, being near the close of his term, was unwilling to bring possible embarrassment upon his successor by inaugurating a policy that the latter might not desire to carry out. Hence the matter was turned over to the Wilson administration.

It cannot be doubted that the attitude of the United States embarrassed General Huerta in his relations with other foreign governments, and tended to aid his enemies at home as well as abroad. Still, our State Department refused to perform the much desired act. Secretary Knox's letter to Mr. Wilson, February 21, 1913, appears to give an insight into the whole situation:

The Department is disposed to consider the new Provisional Government as being legally established and to believe it apparently intends to reestablish peace and order throughout Mexico and to hope that it has the support of the majority of the Mexican people. It will, however, be evident to those now in responsible control in Mexico that, especially in view of the situation which has prevailed for the past two years or more, this government must very carefully consider the question of their ability and earnest disposition to comply with rules of international law and comity, the obligations of treaties, and the general duties to foreigners and foreign governments incident to international intercourse.

You are instructed, therefore, to say to those seeking recognition as the new Provisional Government that the government of the United States will be glad to receive assurances that the outstanding questions between this country and Mexico, which, among other things, have done so much to mar the relations between the two Governments, which should be so especially friendly, will be dealt with in a satisfactory manner. . . .

That the administration of justice throughout Mexico shall be raised to such a plane that this government will no longer be compelled by manifestly unfair and unproper actions on the part of certain Mexican courts, to make diplomatic representations in favor of its unjustly treated nationals;

And finally, but most important, that the Mexican Government agree in principle to the settlement of all claims resulting from the loss of life by American citizens and damages to American property, on account of the recent political disturbances in Mexico by presentation thereof to a mixed international commission which shall award damages. . . .[13]

---

accredited here, but two, accord official recognition to the present Provisional Government." For. Rel., p. 807, Wilson to Bryan, June 9, 1913.

[13] Ibid., pp. 728-729, Knox to Wilson, February 21, 1913.

Seven days later, Knox wrote:

Any formal act of recognition is to be avoided just at present. In the meantime, this Government is considering the question in the light of the usual tests applied to such cases, important among which is the question of degree to which the population of Mexico assents to the new regime and the question of disposition and ability to protect foreigners and their interests and to respond to all international obligations. . . . The Department realizes, of course, that the paramount interests of the government of the United States, namely, the safety of American citizens and their interests in Mexico, must be respected.[14]

When the Wilson Administration came into power, March 4, 1913, Mr. Henry Lane Wilson continued to work faithfully for the recognition of Huerta. He did not, however, advocate recognition of the Provisional Government until that government should demonstrate ability to restore and establish peace and order throughout the Republic and could guarantee protection to the lives and property of foreigners. This Wilson expected to see soon established. He said, " The question of our recognition, therefore, would appear to depend more upon expediency and interest than upon correct procedure, and I believe that it should be considered entirely from those viewpoints." [15]   Henry Lane Wilson gave legal justification for Huerta's assumption of power in a despatch dated March 12, arguing that upon the death of Madero, Lascurain, Minister of Foreign Relations, immediately took the oath as Provisional President under the Constitution. A new Secretary of Foreign Relations, was not appointed, but General Huerta was made Secretary of Gobernación. With the resignation of Lascurain, the Presidency naturally devolved upon Huerta, and he took the oath of office as President of the Republic.[16]

In the same despatch Mr. Wilson mentioned the fact that the new government needed the support of the United States in order that it might be sustained and strengthened. He asserted that many other nations withheld recognition from

---

[14] Ibid., p. 748, Knox to Wilson, February 28, 1913.
[15] Ibid., p. 773.
[16] Ibid., p. 772, Wilson to Bryan, March 12, 1913.

Mexico, awaiting the action of the United States,[17] that our attitude should take on a color of constructive sympathy instead of conspiring against the reestablishment of order and peace in a neighboring republic. The financial situation, too, which was at the time pressing and urgent, could not be solved by the procurement of the necessary loans while the question of legitimacy and constitutionality of the government was in doubt.[18]

President Wilson's policy of "hands-off" was definitely stated in an address before a joint session of the two Houses of Congress, August 27, 1913. To quote:

What is it our duty to do? Clearly, everything that we do must be rooted in patience and done with calm and disinterested deliberation. Impatience on our part would be childish, and would be fraught with every risk of wrong and folly. We can afford to exercise the self-restraint of a really great nation which realizes its own strength and scorns to misuse it. It was our duty to offer our active assistance. It is now our duty to show what true neutrality will do to enable the people of Mexico to set their affairs in order again and wait for a further opportunity to offer our friendly counsels. . . . I shall follow the best practice of nations in the matter of neutrality by forbidding the exportation of arms or munitions of war of any kind from the United States to any part of the Republic of Mexico. . . .[19]

As the President looked upon it, the material interests of the country wished him to recognize Huerta and would sanction such an act for the sake of securing the dividends of oil and mining companies, without regard for the rights of mil-

---

[17] Later Henry Lane Wilson in a despatch to Mr. Bryan, dated May 17, 1913, said that the principal European and South American countries had accorded recognition to Huerta. (For. Rel., 1913, pp. 804-807.) Mr. Langhlin (American Chargé d'affaires at London) in a letter to Mr. Bryan, July 11, 1913, remarked in the following manner: "Sir Edward Grey has made to me the strange but definite statement that the recognition of the Government of Mexico by the British Government was provisional and would terminate in October at the Mexican election, when the question of recognition would come up *de novo*. He said other European Governments' recognition was similarly provisional. He expressed the hope that United States might see way to give additional strength emanating from similar recognition. I should like to know whether or not there is any information on the subject you wish to convey informally." For. Rel., 1913, p. 811.

[18] Ibid., p. 773.

[19] Messages and Papers of the Presidents, XVI, 7887-7888.

lions of Mexican people.[20]   He said, " I have to pause and
remind myself that I am President of the United States and
not of a small group of Americans with vested interests in
Mexico." [21]

Huerta refused to conclude any of the pending questions
between the two countries, or to settle the special or general
claims cases until recognition was granted his government.[22]
This President Wilson refused to give.   As a result Henry
Lane Wilson was called to Washington for a conference. This
was followed by his resignation.[23]   In August, John Lind,
former Governor of Minnesota, was sent to Mexico City as the
special agent of President Wilson.[24]   The President was of
the opinion that the time had come when the policy of
" hands-off," announced in March, should give way to an
offer to assist Mexico out of her difficulties.   In making this
change, he was careful to emphasize the earlier assurance
that the United States was acting in the spirit of disinterested friendship.   The reason for his change he stated
thus:

The present situation in Mexico is incompatible with the fulfillment
of international obligations on the part of Mexico, with the civilized
development of Mexico herself, and with the maintenance of toler-
able political and economic conditions in Central America.[25]

Through Mr. Lind, the President extended the following
terms of settlement:

(1) An immediate cessation of fighting throughout Mexico, a def-
        inite armistice solemnly entered into and scrupulously ob-
        served;
(2) Security given for an early and free election in which all will
        agree to take part;
(3) The consent of General Huerta to bind himself not to be a can-

---

[20] There was also much opposition to Huerta within the United
States as well as in Mexico. See For. Rel., 1913, pp. 747-750.
[21] J. B. Scott, President Wilson's Foreign Policy, p. 383.
[22] For. Rel., 1913, Mr. Wilson to Mr. Bryan, May 8, 1913, p. 799.
At this time the Chamizal and Colorado River cases were pending
as well as the general claims which had existed between the two
countries since 1867.
[23] For. Rel., 1913, p. 817.
[24] Ibid., p. 818.
[25] Ibid., p. 822.

didate for election as President of the Republic at this election; and

(4) The agreement of all parties to abide by the results of the election and cooperate in the most loyal way in organizing and supporting the new administration.[26]

Mr. Lind executed his difficult mission with tact and good judgment.[27] He made clear to the authorities in Mexico City not only the purpose of his visit but the spirit in which it had been undertaken.[28] Nevertheless, General Huerta rejected the proposals which he submitted.[29]

Now relations between the two governments showed little change until about the middle of October, when the Washington government found it expedient to notify General Huerta that the United States had no intention of recognizing his claim to the Presidency, even though the election then in progress should result in his favor. The elections held under the Huerta régime were not the orderly processes of constitutional government which the President found essential to the restoration of normal conditions.[30]

The recognition of Huerta was not to remain a debatable question for long, because the reform elements in the northern States were soon to revolt again, and the world was

[26] Ibid.

[27] Edgar E. Robinson and Victor J. West, The Foreign Policy of Woodrow Wilson, 1913-1917, p. 192.

[28] For a critique of President Wilson's Policy, see Henry Lane Wilson, Diplomatic Episodes in Mexico, Belgium and Chile, chs. xliv and xlv.

[29] Ibid., pp. 823-827, Reply of the Secretary of Foreign Affairs, Señor Gamboa, to the proposals of the American Government.

[30] Ibid., p. 838, Bryan to the Mexican Foreign Office, October 13, 1913. " The President, shocked at the lawless methods employed by General Huerta and as a sincere friend of Mexico, is deeply distressed by the present situation. General Huerta's course in dissolving Congress and arresting deputies, the President finds it impossible to regard otherwise than as an act of bad faith towards the United States. It is not only a violation of constitutional guarantees, but it destroys all possibility of a free and fair election. The President believes that an election held at this time and under conditions as they now exist would have none of the sanctions with which the law surrounds the ballot, and that its results could therefore not be regarded as representing the will of the people. The President would not feel justified in accepting the result of such an election or in recognizing a President so chosen."

to hear of Venustiano Carranza and the Constitutionalists. By December 1913, they controlled the entire North and were gradually pressing southward. Carranza's democratic ideas followed his flag. He confiscated and divided many large estates, selling portions of them on easy terms to the poorer classes.[31]

In February 1914, the revolutionists captured Mazatlan, and by April 8 they had reached Tampico. Five days later, that city fell into their hands. During the attack, the United States became more deeply involved in Mexican affairs than she had anticipated.[32]

The position of Huerta gradually became more difficult. Foreign recognition and financial support were withheld. Meanwhile the forces of Carranza and Villa[33] were regularly winning victories. On July 15, 1914, Huerta resigned and left Mexico on a German warship bound for Europe. The Minister of Foreign Relations, Dr. Francisco Carbajal, automatically became President[34] and served for nearly a month,

---

[31] See Herbert I. Priestly, The Mexican Nation, ch. xxv.

[32] The arrest of American sailors by Huerta's soldiers in Tampico April 9, 1914, was followed by Huerta's refusal to accede to the demands which the United States considered essential for atonement for the injury received by us. Determined " to compel the recognition of the dignity of the United States," President Wilson finally asked Congress for its approval to use armed force. But before receiving the acquiescence of Congress to such an act, he took steps which by April 22 resulted in the complete occupation of Vera Cruz.

Before the marines were replaced by the regular soldiers in that city, the President accepted the offer of the three Latin American Governments of Argentina, Brazil, and Chile which had tendered their good offices in an effort to end the dispute. The conference of mediation, having convened at Niagara Falls on May 20, remained in session for six weeks. It finally adjourned without having arrived at any immediate successful results, but it was followed by the elimination of Huerta, who resigned, July 15, 1914, and fled from the country. On August 20, General Carranza, whose authority had been disputed by General Francisco Villa, gained control at the capital. Carranza promised to protect American citizens and their property rights in Mexico, whereupon the United States forces were withdrawn from Vera Cruz in November, 1914. (See Latané, A History of American Foreign Policy, pp. 671-673; also, American Journal of International Law, VIII, 483.)

[33] In former years Francisco Villa had been a bandit, but now he became the leader of Carranza's armed forces.

[34] For. Rel., 1914, Brazilian Minister Cardoso De Oliveira to Mexico to the Secretary of State, July 15, 1914.

when the approach of Carranza's forces caused him to dissolve the government and abandon the city. General Carranza entered the capital August 20, 1914.[35]

The Wilson administration justified itself for withholding recognition from the Huerta Government for the following reasons: (1) the fate of Madero, (2) the failure to hold a real election, and (3) the fact that Huerta was not in control of the larger part of the country. In his address before the Senate July 19, 1922, Senator E. F. Ladd said:

Our previous refusals to recognize foreign governments usually have been based upon the conditions surrounding their origin. It was the illegality and violence attending the overthrow of Madero by General Huerta that caused President Wilson to withhold recognition in that case.[36]

To have recognized Huerta would have meant the same as announcing to all ambitious military leaders that they need only ally themselves with a strong force, murder or drive the lawful rulers from the country, and establish a supreme military dictatorship in order to gain the support of the United States. This President Wilson refused to do.[37]

Within a month after Carranza entered Mexico City, Villa was in open revolt against him. Exactly what the latter desired is exceedingly difficult to say, for he denied presidential ambitions. On the other hand, it is apparent that Carranza wished to be chosen President in an election; therefore, he was careful to shun the office of Provisional President. A convention of constitutionalist leaders met and chose General Eulalio Gutiérrez for that office.[38] Carranza at once refused to approve of this selection, maintaining that his wishes had not been complied with. Gutiérrez appointed Villa Com-

---

[35] Priestly, ch. xxvi.

[36] 67th Cong., 2d sess., Congressional Record, Vol. 62, pp. 10417-10426, Edwin F. Ladd, Recognition of the Mexican Government, speech in the Senate, July 19, 1922.

[37] For a criticism of Wilson's policy toward Mexico, see the editorials entitled "Exit Huerta" and "Again the Big Policeman," in the Nation, XCIX, 91.

[38] For. Rel., 1914, p. 620, Special agent Canove to the Secretary of State, November 13, 1914.

mander-in-Chief of all the forces and Carranza lost little time in withdrawing from Mexico City.

Just at this time the United States saw fit to withdraw her troops from Vera Cruz, November 23, 1914, after about seven months' occupation.[39] Carranza at once transferred his government to Vera Cruz and continued the struggle under the leadership of General Obregón.

In January of 1915, the Constitutionalist convention deposed Provisional President Gutiérrez and appointed Colonel Rogue Gonzales Garza to succeed him.[40] Garza ruled for ten days and then fled before Carranza's forces. Later, in June, 1915, the convention deposed Garza and chose Francisco Lagos Chazaro for the presidential office.[41] In the meantime, General Obregón's victories over Villa continued; yet, none was decisive.

By this time, President Wilson believed that the situation demanded action on the behalf of the United States. June 2, 1915, he called upon the factions in Mexico to act together promptly for the relief of their country, otherwise the United States would employ means to help Mexico save herself.[42]

Apparently the President carried out his threat, for in the closing session of the Pan-American Conference, October 9, 1915, it was agreed that the Carranza organization constituted a "de facto" government and its recognition was recommended.[43] The United States formally granted "de facto" recognition October 19, 1915,[44] following this action the next

---

[39] Above, note 30.

[40] For. Rel., 1915, p. 645, Vice Consul Silliman to Mr. Bryan January 16, 1915.

[41] Ibid., p. 717, Special agent G. C. Carothers to Mr. Lansing, June 19, 1915.

[42] Ibid., 1915, p. 695.

[43] Secretary Lansing, Ambassadors of Argentina, Brazil, Chile, and Ministers from Bolivia, Uruguay, and Guatemala went into conference on October 9, 1915. The result of the conference was given to the press in the following statement: "The Conferences, after careful consideration of the facts, have found that the carrancista party is the only party possessing the essentials for recognition as the *de facto* government of Mexico, and they have so reported to their respective Governments." For. Rel., 1915, p. 767.

[44] Ibid., p. 771. Lansing to Arredondo (confidential agent of the "de facto" government in Mexico) October 19, 1915. It seems that

day by an embargo on the shipment of arms to all anti-government parties in Mexico.[45] Thus normal relations were restored between the United States and Mexico.[46] However, " de jure " recognition was not given Carranza until March 3, 1917, when the American Ambassador H. P. Fletcher presented his credentials. The fact that Carranza was not duly declared elected until later [47] leads one to believe that again, perhaps, expediency played a part in our actions. At this time the central powers of Europe were holding the attention of the entire world.

Carranza claimed to have control of twenty-four of the twenty-seven states of Mexico. He guaranteed the protection of the lives and property of foreigners and the payment of just indemnities for damages incurred during the recent troubles. All treaties with other nations were to be carried out. In addition Carranza promised land reform, the development of education, and an effective elective system.[48] With Villa driven back in a succession of defeats, the Pan-American Conference saw no better course than to accept these promises and guarantees. Carranza was given a chance.

The Wilson administration was to be once again compelled to meet a change in Mexican affairs. President Carranza was forced out of office by General Obregón and his allies. The

---

President Wilson was simply attempting to help Mexico by granting recognition at this time. General Carranza was unable to maintain order throughout the country. Villa refused to believe himself beaten, and the recognized government did not occupy the capital at the time, nor was Carranza duly elected until March 12, 1917. Ibid., 1917, p. 910.

[45] Ibid., 1915, p. 772, a Proclamation.

[46] It is interesting to note that according to Colonel House, Wilson and he had agreed that " if Carranza was to be recognized he must first guarantee religious freedom, give amnesty for all political offences, institute the land reforms that had been promised, give protection to foreigners, and recognize their just claims." C. Seymour, The Intimate Papers of Colonel House, I, 224. The New York Evening World expressed the opinion, " Instead of forcing Mexico to take what we thought good for her, we have in general council singled out the man and the party who seem nearest to expressing her somewhat mussed-up ideal."

[47] For. Rel., 1917, p. 938.

[48] For. Rel., 1915, p. 763. E. Arrendondo to Secretary of State, October 7, 1915.

latter entered Mexico City May 8, 1920, but did not take the oath of office until late in November of the same year. To fill the unexpired term of Carranza, Adolfo de la Huerta was chosen substitute President by the reorganized Congress. He served until November 30, 1920, when General Obregón took office.[49] Obregón was elected President September 8, 1920, by an overwhelming majority. At this election military force was entirely absent and not one single instance of disorder at the polls was reported.[50]

Although General Obregón was chosen in a duly conducted election, his government was not recognized by that of the United States for a period of over two years. During this time it was the desire of the Mexican Government to secure the recognition without yielding to the demand that American lives and property rights be guaranteed by treaty as a previous condition. Such a treaty General Obregón held beyond his competency to sign, alleging that it would give greater security to foreigners than to Mexicans.

Now, as was the case with General Huerta, President Wilson's policy was one of "watchful waiting." He announced his policy in the following words: " The policy of the United States to Mexico is a policy of hope and helpfulness; it is a policy of Mexico for the Mexicans. That, after all, is the traditional policy of this country. . . ."[51]

On the other hand, there was much opposition to the President's announced policy. The States of Arizona, California, Illinois, Michigan, Texas, and Oklahoma officially requested of the Washington Government the resumption of formal relations between the two countries. The chambers of commerce of cities like St. Louis, Los Angeles, and San Francisco, after a thorough investigation by various trade representatives in Mexico, likewise advised the same steps. Individuals like William R. Hearst [52] and Samuel Gompers were

---

[49] For a more detailed account read Herbert I. Priestly, ch. xxvii.
[50] Congressional Record, 67th Cong., 2d sess., Vol. 62, No. 86, p. 4957.
[51] James B. Scott, President Wilson's Foreign Policy, p. 392.
[52] New York Cosmopolitan Book Corporation, 1922, p. 37.

continually using their power and influence in Mexico's behalf. The latter contended that the only persons who could conceivably derive advantage from the continued withholding of recognition were certain American bankers who hoped to drive better bargains with Mexico by creating the impression that they had some influence in determining the matter of recognition.[53]

Senator Ladd, in his speech before the Senate July 19, 1922, commented upon the subject in the following manner:

It is my contention that the executive branch of the government has no right to withhold arbitrarily recognition from a friendly republic, when that republic for more than two years had proved beyond all reasonable question that it was established in accordance to its own constitutional provisions and international law; that it is founded on support; that it offers all reasonable safeguards to life and property rights of its own citizens and foreign nationals; that it accepts all valid international obligations; that it advocates no confiscatory principles; and whose only offense is to insist upon certain sovereign rights which are expressly safeguarded in a treaty concluded with Mexico by our Government which has been revoked.[54] It is noteworthy in this respect that the reason officially given out by our Department of State for failure to recognize Obregón has never even by implication accused him of complicity in the death of Carranza. Before the bar of public opinion, both in Mexico and abroad, he stands universally acquitted of this heinous crime.[55]

President Obregón repeatedly announced that it was his determination to pay all foreign damage claims.[56] In pursuit of this policy, he issued a decree, July 12, 1921, directing all Mexican diplomatic agents in foreign countries to call attention to the various governments where they were stationed that the Republic of Mexico would enter into arrangements with those governments to adjust the claims of any foreigners who had suffered damage by reason of revolution.[57]

Secretary of State Hughes' attitude towards Mexico may be seen from the following statement:

---

[53] American Federationist, March 1922, XXIX, 197-199.
[54] Congressional Record, Vol. 62, pp. 10417-10426, Edwin F. Ladd's Speech in the Senate, July 19, 1922.
[55] Ibid.
[56] Current History, August 1, 1922, XVI, 911.
[57] Ladd's Speech before Senate, July 19, 1922, Congressional Record, Vol. 62, pp. 10417-10426.

Whenever Mexico is ready to give assurances that she will perform
her fundamental obligations in the protection both of persons and
property validly acquired there will be no obstacles to the most
advantageous relations between the two peoples.[58]

Again, he made the statement:

The question of recognition is a subordinate one, but there will be
no difficulty as to this, for if General Obregon is ready to negotiate
a proper treaty, it to be drawn so as to be negotiated with him, and
the making of the treaty in the proper form will accomplish the
recognition of the government that makes it. In short, when it
appears that there is a government in Mexico willing to bind itself
to the discharge of primary international obligations, concurrently
with that act its recognition will take place. This government
desires immediate and cordial relations of mutual helpfulness, and
simply wishes that the basis of international intercourse should be
properly maintained.[59]

From what we have said, it seems that the United States
made it clear to President Obregón that if Mexico was to be
recognized she must protect and respect the property of the
United States citizens who had bought land in Mexico,
whether for use or speculation.

In the Recognition Conference between the United States
delegates, Charles B. Warren and John B. Payne, and the
Mexicans, Ramón Ross and Fernando Gonzalez Rosa, the
following points were discussed: (1) claims of the United
States citizens against Mexico, (2) payment of interest on
the foreign debt, (3) restoration of the railroads to their
lawful private owners, (4) proposed partition of the large
estates, (5) taxation of oil leases and oil exports, (6) retroactive features of Article XXVII of the Constitution of 1917
which proposed to nationalize the land and subsoil resources
of Mexico. The important thing to notice here is that the
United States stressed economic imperialism. President Obregón might have been recognized as soon as he had demon-
strated his ability to maintain order and a disposition to live
up to ordinary international obligations, leaving American
vested interests to work out their own salvation. The State
Department chose instead to champion the cause of the agents
of imperialism, giving their demands an official tone and

---

[58] Ibid.   [59] Ibid.

attempting to force Mexican concessions in consideration for the granting of recognition.[60]

The Harding-Coolidge administrations, heirs to President Wilson's Mexican policy, proposed that a treaty of amity and commerce be negotiated which would settle the points of dispute between the governments and offered recognition as the price for such a treaty.[61] The Mexican Government refused to accept recognition on such terms, as it felt it would be placed in the position of an inferior agreeing to commands.[62]

President Obregón stated definitely that Mexico should never buy recognition at the cost of sacrificing her Constitution; consequently there was no yielding on this point.[63] But eventually a compromise was reached, and while not yielding on the principles of Article 27, President Obregón gave assurance that personal permits for drilling would be issued in cases covered by the controversy. The United States Commissioners, while accepting this arrangement, reserved all the rights of their position.[64]

Finally, it was agreed that two Mixed Claims Commissions should be created for the purpose of adjusting, in accordance with the principles of international law, all outstanding claims of Americans for damages suffered during the Mexican revolutions, and also for the settlement of Mexican claims against the United States.[65]

The three steps by which the Mexican Government pro-

---

[60] See Laswell, "Political Policies and the International Investment Market," in The Journal of Political Economy, June, 1923, XXXI, 380-400; Chamberlin, "Property Rights under the New Mexican Constitution," Political Science Quarterly, September, 1917, XXXII.

[61] Secretary Fall declared: "So long as I have anything to do with Mexico, no government in Mexico will be recognized, with my consent, which government does not first enter a written agreement practically along the lines suggested, namely the recommendation of the Fall report." Senator Ladd's Speech before Senate, July 19, 1922.

[62] Current History, December 1923, p. 391.

[63] New York Times, May 21, 1921.

[64] See Current History, December 1923, p. 391.

[65] The New York Times, August 31, 1923.

posed to adjust the differences and restore formal diplomatic relations with the United States were:

(1) The signing of a special convention for the purpose of adjudicating claims of citizens of the United States against Mexico that had arisen during the revolution,

(2) the implicit recognition of the Obregon Government by that of the United States, and

(3) the signing of a general claims convention for the purpose of adjudicating the claims of either country with regard to the other that were not covered by the special claims convention.[66]

On July 27, 1923, the texts of both the general and the special Claims Conventions were formally approved by the joint commissioners. Subsequently, the statements and recommendations of the United States Commissioners and those of the Mexican Commissioners were approved by President Coolidge and President Obregón, respectively. On the basis of the understanding thus reached by the executives, the United States formally accorded recognition to the Obregón Government August 31, 1923.[67] The special Claims Convention provided for the adjudication of claims of American citizens who suffered losses or damages during the period from 1910 to 1920. The General Commission was to settle claims of the citizens of either country originating between July 4, 1868, and, the date of the termination of the said commission. Thus, with the signing of the above mentioned convention in September 1923, the slate was wiped clean of all questions at issue between the two countries.

The reasons given by the State Department for not recognizing the Obregón Government sooner were:

(1) The Government was founded on violence;

(2) Mexico was too unsettled to offer guarantees of security;

(3) Guarantees must be given that Article Twenty-Seven of the Constitution of 1917 should not be retroactive in its application.[68]

The extension of recognition by the United States to Presi-

---

[66] Charles W. Hackett, " The Mexican Revolution and the United States, 1910-1926," World Peace Foundation Pamphlets (1926, IX, 354).

[67] The New York Times, August 31, 1923. For discussion of claims see Congressional Record, Vol. 65, Part II, pp. 1322-1324.

[68] Current History, December 1923, p. 391.

dent Obregón meant that the former was convinced of the
good faith of the newly established government and indicated
that a satisfactory understanding had been reached on all
points of controversy that had previously existed.

Finally, to quote the New York Times: " Recognition has
come about without any abandonment of fundamental principles laid down by either side. Secretary Hughes only
sought to be assured that American rights and interests would
not be endangered." [69]

The instant case is very similar to that of 1845 and 1846,
as in that crisis the policy of the United States was to drive
the Mexican Government into a dilemma. If Obregón should
have signed the treaty demanded, he would have become the
victim of his political enemies, who could have inflamed the
national pride of the Mexican people against an unworthy
President who had been guilty of betraying his country to
greedy neighbors. Again, should he not have signed the
treaty, he would have been unable to continue his work of
reform or to meet the obligations of his country. It will be
remembered that his announced policy was to finance national
progress through the natural resources and that the reserve
derived from oil taxes was to be applied to the debt. In
1845-46, President Polk had maintained that the United
States was making every effort to prevent war, but war came
because the Mexican Government refused to negotiate on our
terms. The instant situation, then, like that of 1845-46, was
settled only when Mexico agreed that two Mixed Claims
Commissions should be created for the purpose of adjusting,
in accordance with the principles of international law, all
outstanding claims existing between citizens of the two countries. It seems that the Department of State was over-zealous
in demanding protection of American property rights in
Mexico.

The Government of Mexico passed on November 30, 1924,
from the hands of General Alvaro Obregón, the retiring President, into those of General Plutarco Elias Calles, who had

---

[69] The New York Times, September 2, 3, 1923.

been chosen President of the Republic in the election of July 6. This was an event of overshadowing interest and importance in Mexico's history. The peaceful transmission of executive power from a retiring constitutional Mexican President to his constitutionally elected successor, until the present, had occurred only three other times since the independence of Mexico; namely, in 1851 when Arista succeeded Herrera; in 1880 when Gonzales succeeded Diaz; and in 1884 when Diaz succeeded Gonzales.

In the case of President Calles as in each succeeding change in government, the United States was satisfied to accept the rightful choice of the Mexican people. At the same time it should be remembered that recognition did not automatically solve all the questions which are likely to arise between the two neighboring States, which differ so greatly in both race and customs.

CONCLUSION

On account of the kaleidoscopic rapidity with which Mexico's chieftains have succeeded one another at the Capital, it has been a rather difficult matter for the United States to maintain what might be termed a consistent policy of recognition. In fact, the writer often doubts if it is not too much to ask that such a policy should exist. On the other hand, there seem to be certain broad principles which have guided our State Department from the first time it was forced to deal with the question of recognizing Mexico in 1822, to the present day.

The American policy, formulated by Jefferson while Secretary of State under Washington, has had its influence upon succeeding administrations. Jefferson gave it vigorous expression in a letter to Charles Pinckney, American minister to the Court of St. James, dated December 30, 1792:

We certainly cannot deny to other nations that principle whereon our own government is founded, that every nation has a right to govern itself internally under what form it pleases and to change these forms at its own will; and externally to transact business through whatever organ it chooses whether that be a King, Convention, Assembly, Committee, President or whatever it be. The only thing essential is the will of the nation.[1]

This was merely the logical conclusion derived from the American Revolution and from Jefferson's theories of government by consent of the governed.

The problem of recognition existed before the days of Jefferson, but it was he who made it a definite question of international law and evolved the theory of " de facto " recognition. This theory forms one of the distinctive contributions of the United States diplomacy to the present international system.

To say that the recognition policy of the United States towards Mexico has been strictly one of " de facto " recognition or one of strict application of the legitimist principle would be false, at least in degree. Instead, it has been a

---

[1] Jefferson's Works (Ford ed.), III, 500.

fundamentally continuous policy, one in which seemingly changed methods of action during special periods have been due to a change in the emphasis or interpretation placed upon the two criteria and perhaps to considerations of the general policy under the demands of the situation.[2] Our policy of recognition has fundamentally from the earliest times until the present rested upon these principles, first, the present and future stability of the government to be recognized, second, the willingness and ability of the government to fulfil its international obligations. The first of these criteria under the guise of a demand for popular sanction of the political organism to be recognized has been applied from the very beginning. The latter criterion, though present probably from the beginning, was not to be emphasized while the foreign policy of the United States was in its earlier stages, but was to receive increasing attention with the extension of American interests towards the south.

With the growth of American interests in foreign lands, there has been an accompanying practice of our State Department to put special emphasis in recognition cases upon the government's ability to meet its international responsibilities. Our policy towards Mexico has not proved the exception to the rule in this particular. The sympathy that was so predominant in the first case of recognition appears soon to have given way to an interest that was chiefly economic and expedient in nature.

To reiterate, it seems that during the first half of the nineteenth century, in the policy of recognition of the United States towards new governments in Mexico, emphasis was placed on the latter's power to maintain control and support

---

Charles C. Tansill, " War Powers of the President of the United States with Special Reference to the Beginning of Hostilities," Political Science Quarterly (March 1930). To quote: " A careful examination of documentary material, however, clearly indicates that there has been no deviation for any great moment in the American policy of recognition from 1789 to the present time. All that Mr. Seward and Mr. Wilson did was to give unmistakable clarity to the American position, and to make explicit what has always been implied in the stand America has taken."

of the governed. Since that time other elements in the matter of recognition have been stressed by the United States, particularly the disposition of the new government to adhere to the obligations of treaties and international friendship. Similar principles have been followed in the matter of the recognition of Colombia in 1900, of Haiti in 1911, and in the question of the recognition of the Chinese Republic in 1913. President Coolidge refused to accord recognition to new governments in certain Central American states unless the new governments had come into existence by constitutional means.[3]

. As for the influence of the Monroe Doctrine upon our recognition policy towards Mexico, we have only one outstanding case from which to judge, namely Maximilian's attempt to establish an Empire there. Secretary Seward, it is true, opposed foreign intervention from the beginning, and recognition was withheld from the Austrian Archduke; yet, in this case, as in all other instances, outside events deterred the United States from using armed force to defend her doctrine.

As we have seen, Seward and others emphasized as the test for recognition the ability of new governments to fulfil their international obligations. According to President Wilson, a government created by force, in violation of a democratic constitution under which political changes can be brought about by peaceful means, ought not to be recognized.[4] Wilson perhaps went a step in advance of Lincoln's Secretary in considering the interests of the whole world as well as those of the United States. Yet, in his dealings with the Huerta government he simply applied the traditional test of " popular approval " and " ability to fulfil international obligations." He followed then a policy long fixed by precedent.

As a concluding word it seems apparent from this study that after all, internal problems are in many instances inter-

---

[3] Conference on Central American Affairs, Washington, December 4, 1922-February 7, 1923, pp. 288-289.
[4] See: E. E. Robinson and V. J. West, The Foreign Policy of Woodrow Wilson, pp. 179-180; Scott, President Wilson's Foreign Policy, pp. 231-232; Hyde, International Law, I, 73.

national problems, and vice versa; that perhaps such a thing as a carefully observed foreign policy has not been followed for any great period of time by the United States towards Mexico; but that there have been certain guiding principles which have been practised and adhered to, their emphasis depending in a large measure upon time and circumstances.

APPENDIX

First Period

First Regency........September 28, 1821, to April 11, 1822.

Second Regency.......April 11, 1822, to May 18, 1822.

Augustine I, Emperor..Proclaimed May 18, 1822; took oath May 31; crowned July 21, 1822; abdicated March 19, 1823.

Provisional
Government.........The Marqués of Vivanco, political chief of Mexico, took charge on the abdication of Iturbide. On March 31, 1823, Congress elected a Supreme Executive Council of three, which entered upon its duties on April 2, 1823.

Under Constitution of October 4, 1824

President.............General Guadaloupe Victoria, October 10, 1824, to April 1, 1829.

President.............General Vicente Guerrero, April 1, 1829, to December 17, 1829.

Acting President......Licentiate José María de Brocanegra, December 17, 1829, to December 23, 1829.

Supreme Executive
Council ....December 23, 1829, to December 31, 1829.

President.............General Anastasio Bustamante, December 31, 1829, to August 14, 1832.

Acting President......General Melchor Muzquez, August 14, 1832, to December 24, 1832.

President.............General Manuel Gómez Pedraza, December 24, 1832, to April 1, 1833.

President.............General Antonio López de Santa Anna, April 1, 1833, to January 28, 1835.

President.............General Miguel Barragan, from January 28, 1835, to February 27, 1836.

President.............Licentiate José Justo Carro, February 27, 1836, to April 19, 1837.

Under Constitution of January 1, 1837

President.............General Anastasio Bustamante, April 19, 1837, to March 18, 1839.
On the latter date Bustamante was replaced by Santa Anna. From July 10 to July 17, 1839, General Nicolás Bravo ácted as President. Bustamante was in charge from July 17, 1839, to September 22, 1841, when Don Javier Echeverria was installed as Acting President.

---

[1] The Mexican Year Book (1920-1921). Ed. by Robert G. Cleland.

Dictatorship

Provisional President..General Antonio López de Santa Anna, October 10, 1841, to October 26, 1842.

Substitute President...General Nicolás Bravo, October 26, 1842, to March 5, 1843.

Provisional President..General Antonio López de Santa Anna, March 5, 1843, to October 4, 1843.

Substitute President...General Valentin Canalizo, October 4, 1843, to February 1, 1844.

Substitute President...General Valentin Canalizo, February 1, 1844, to June 4, 1844.

(Canalizo during this period was acting in lieu of Santa Anna, who had been elected Constitutional President, under the law of June 12, 1843.)

Under Constitution of June 12, 1843

President.............General Antonio López de Santa Anna, June 4, 1844, to September 12, 1844.

Acting President......General José Joaquin de Herrera, September 12, 1844, to September 21, 1844.

Acting President......General Valentin Canalizo, September 21, 1844, to December 6, 1844.

President.............General José Joaquin de Herrera, December 6, 1844, to December 30, 1845.

President.............General Mariano Paredes y Arrillaga, January 4, 1846, to July 28, 1846.

President.............General Nicolás Bravo, July 28, 1844, to August 4, 1846.

Acting President......General José Mariano Salas, August 5, 1846, to December 24, 1846. By decree of August 22, 1846, the Constitution of 1824 was reestablished.

Under Constitution of 1824

Vice-President and
  Acting President....Don Valentin Gomez Farias, December 24, 1846, to March 21, 1847.

President.............General Antonio López de Santa Anna, March 22, 1847, to April 1, 1847.

Substitute President..General Pedro M. Anaya, April 1, 1847, to May 20, 1847.

President.............General Antonio López de Santa Anna, May 20, 1847, to September 16, 1847.

President.............Licentiate Manuel de la Peña y Peña, September 16, 1847, to November 14, 1847.

Acting President......General Pedro M. Anaya, November 14, 1847, to January 8, 1848.

President and
  Acting President....Don Manuel de la Peña y Peña, January 8, 1848, to June 2, 1848.

President.............General José Joaquin de Herrera, June 2, 1848, to January 15, 1851.

President.............General Mariano Arista, January 15, 1851, to January 5, 1853.

Acting President......Don Juan B. Ceballos, January 5, 1853, to February 7, 1853.

Dictatorship

President with
Full Powers........General Antonio López de Santa Anna, April
20, 1853, to August 11, 1855.

Governments Subsequent to the Revolution of Ayutla

Acting President......General Martin Carrera, August 14, 1855, to
September 12, 1855.
In charge of Federal
District...........General Romulo Diaz de la Vega, September
12, 1855, to October 4, 1855.
Acting President......General Juan Alvarez, October 4, 1855, to
December 9, 1855.
Substitute President...General Ignacio Comonfort, December 11,
1855, to December 1, 1857.
President............General Ignacio Comonfort, December 1, 1857,
to December 19, 1857.
Provisional President..Benito Juárez, December 19, 1857, to June 15,
1861.
President............Benito Juárez, June 15, 1861, to November 8,
1865.   1861-1867, period of French Inter-
vention and of Maximilian.
President............Benito Juárez, November 8, 1865, to Decem-
ber 25, 1867.
President............Benito Juárez, December 25, 1867, to Decem-
ber 1, 1871.
President............Benito Juárez, December 1, 1871, to July 18,
1872. (Died in office.)
President............Sebastian Lerdo de Tejada, July 18, 1872, to
December 1, 1872.
President............Sebastian Lerdo de Tejada, December 1, 1872,
to November 21, 1876.
Provisional President..General Porfirio Diaz, November 28, 1876, to
December 6, 1876.
In charge of the
Executive Power....General Juan N. Mendez, December 6, 1876, to
February 16, 1877.
Provisional President..General Porfirio Diaz, February 16, 1877, to
May 5, 1877.
President............General Porfirio Diaz, May 5, 1877, to Novem-
ber 30, 1880.
President............General Manuel González, December 1, 1880,
to November 30, 1884.
President............General Porfirio Diaz, December 1, 1884, to
November 30, 1888.
President............General Porfirio Diaz, December 1, 1888, to
November 30, 1892.
President............General Porfirio Diaz, December 1, 1892, to
November 30, 1896.
President............General Porfirio Diaz, December 1, 1896, to
November 30, 1900.
President............General Porfirio Diaz, December 1, 1900, to
November, 1904.
President............General Porfirio Diaz, December 1, 1904, to
November 30, 1910.
President............General Porfirio Diaz, December 1, 1910, to
May 25, 1911.

Since the overthrow of Diaz, the following have exercised executive power, though frequently their claims to the office have not been admitted by the country generally or recognized by other nations.

Francisco Leon de la Barra, May 25, 1911, to November 10, 1911.

Francisco Madero, November 10, 1911, to February 19, 1913.

Pedro Lascurain, from 7 p. m. to 7.46 p. m., February 19, 1913.

Victoriano Huerta, February 19, 1913, to August 13, 1914.

Eulalio Gutierrez, December 13, 1914, to January 25, 1915.

Roque González Garza, January 30, 1915, to May 1915.

Francisco Lagos Cházaro, July 31, 1915, to October, 1915.

Venustiano Carranza, March 11, 1917; assassinated May 21, 1920.

Adolfo de la Huerta, President ad interim, June 1 to November 30, 1920.

Alvaro Obregón, December 1, 1920.

1924—Obregón retired and was succeeded by General Calles.

1928—Obregón was reelected President but was assassinated before he could take office. Emilio Portes Gil was chosen provisional President by the National Congress.

Pascual Ortiz Rubio was elected and took office February 5, 1930. He resigned September 3, 1932, and on September 4, Congress elected Gen. Abelardo L. Rodríguez to succeed him.

BIBLIOGRAPHY

I. PRIMARY SOURCES.

   A. United States State Department.
     Despatches—Mexico (1823-1906).
     Instructions—Mexico (1823-1906).
     Miscellaneous Letters (only the letters bearing upon the policy of the United States at certain periods were examined).

   B. Printed Material.
     Annals of Congress (1810-1824).
     American State Papers (1808-1828).
     Congressional Globe (1833-1873).
     Congressional Record (1873-to present).
     Diplomatic Correspondence (1860-1870).
     Foreign Relations (1870-1917).
     Register of Debates (1824-1837).

II. SECONDARY MATERIALS.

   A. Books and Pamphlets.

Adams, Randolph G., A History of the Foreign Policy of the United States (Macmillan Company, 1924).

Bancroft, Frederic, The Life of William H. Seward, Vol. II (Harper Bros., New York and London, 1900).

Blakeslee, George H., Mexico and the Caribbean (New York, 1920).

——, The Recent Foreign Policy of the United States (The Abingdon Press, 1925).

British Year Book of International Law (1921-1922, pp. 57-74).

Buell, Raymond L., The United States and Latin America (Foreign Policy Association, Jan. 1928).

Bulues, Francisco, President Wilson's Responsibility (M. Bulues Book Company, New York, 1916).

——, The Whole Truth About Mexico (M. Bulues Book Company, New York, 1916).

Callahan, James M., The Evolution of Seward's Mexican Policy (Morgantown, West Virginia, 1909).

Chamberlain, George, Is Mexico Worth Saving (The Bobbs-Merril Co., 1922).

Cole, Taylor, The Recognition Policy of the United States Since 1910 (Louisiana State University, 1928).

Colton, Calvin, The Life and Times of Henry Clay (2d ed., New York, 1846).

Corwin, Thomas, The President's Control of Foreign Relations (Washington, 1862).

Dealey, James Q., Foreign Policies of the United States (Ginn and Company, Boston and New York, 1926).

Fenwick, Charles G., International Law (The Century Company, New York and London, 1924).
Fish, Carl R., American Diplomacy (Henry Holt & Co., 1916).
Ford, Paul L., Editor, Jefferson's Writings, Vols. III, VI (G. P. Putnam's Sons, New York, 1892-1899).
———, Writings of Monroe, Vol. VI.
Foster, John W., A Century of American Diplomacy (Boston, 1901).
———, Diplomatic Memoirs, Vol. I (Houghton-Mifflin Co., Boston and New York, 1909).
Garben, P. N., The Gadsden Treaty (Press of the University of Pennsylvania, Philadelphia, 1923).
Garner, James W., American Foreign Policy (New York University Press, New York, 1928).
Goebel, Julius, The Recognition Policy of the United States (edited by the faculty of Political Science of Columbia University, 1915).
Hackett, Charles W., The Mexican Revolution and the United States, 1910-1926 (Boston, World Peace Foundation, 1926).
Hall, William E., International Law (Oxford, 1890).
Hervey, John G., The Legal Effects of Recognition in International Law as Interpreted by the Courts of the United States (Thesis in Political Science at the University of Pennsylvania, 1928).
Hershey, Amos S., The Essentials of International Public Law (The Macmillan Co., New York, 1912).
Hyde, Charles C., International Law, Vol. I (Little, Brown & Co., Boston, 1920).
Johnson, W. F., American Foreign Policy (The Century Company, 1916).
Jones, Chester Lloyd, American Interests in the Caribbean (D. Appleton and Company, 1916).
———, Mexico and its Reconstruction (D. Appleton and Company, 1921).
Koebel, William H., Central America (London, 1917).
Latané, John H., A History of American Foreign Policy (Doubleday, Page & Co., Garden City, New York, 1927).
———, Diplomatic Relations of the United States and Spanish America (Albert Shaw Lectures on Diplomatic History, Baltimore, 1900).
———, The United States and Latin America (Doubleday, Page & Co., 1920).
Manning, William R., Diplomatic Correspondence, 3 vols. (Oxford University Press, 1925).
———, Early Diplomatic Relations between the United States and Mexico (Baltimore, 1916).
Mathews, John M., American Foreign Relations (The Century Co., 1928).
Moore, John B., A Digest of International Law, 8 vols. (Washington, Government Printing Office, 1906).
———, American Diplomacy (Harper & Bros., 1905).

———, History and Digest of International Arbitrations to which the United States has been a Party, 6 vols. (Washington, Government Printing Office, 1898).

———, Editor, The Works of James Buchanan, 12 vols. (J. B. Lippincott Co., Philadelphia and London, 1908-11).

Moyer, George D., Attitude of the United States towards the Recognition of Soviet Russia (Thesis at the University of Pennsylvania, Philadelphia, 1926).

Munro, Dana G., The Five Republics of Central America (Oxford University Press, 1918).

Oppenhein, Lossa F. L., International Law (2d ed., Vol. I, Longmans, Green & Co., 1905-1906).

Paxson, Frederic L., Independence of the South American Republics (Ferris and Leuce, Philadelphia, 1903).

Polks Diary (A. C. McClung and Company, Chicago, 1910).

Priestly, Herbert I., International Relations Pamphlets, Vol. I.

———, The Mexican Nation (The Macmillan Company, 1923).

———, The Mexican Situation (Los Angeles, Cal., 1928).

Rather, Ethel Z., Recognition of the Republic of Texas by the United States (Quarterly of the Texas State Historical Association, 1910).

Reeves, Jesse S., American Diplomacy under Tyler and Polk (The Johns Hopkins Press, Baltimore, 1907).

Rivier, Alphonse, Principles du Droit des Gens (Vol. I, Paris, 1896).

Richardson, James D., Messages and Papers of the Presidents, 10 vols. (Government Printing Office, Washington, 1896-1899).

Rippy, J. Fred, Latin America in World Politics (A. A. Knopf, New York, 1928).

———, Rivalry of the United States and Great Britain over Latin America (Johns Hopkins Press, 1929).

———, The United States and Mexico (A. A. Knopf, New York, 1926).

Rives, George L., The United States and Mexico, 1821-1848, 2 vols. (Scribner's Sons, New York, 1913).

Robertson, William S., History of Latin American Nations (D. Appleton & Co., 1922).

———, Hispanic American Relations with the United States (Oxford University Press, New York, 1923).

———, Rise of the Spanish American Republics (D. Appleton & Co., New York and London, 1918).

Robinson, Edgar E., and West, J. Victor, The Foreign Policy of Woodrow Wilson, 1913-1917 (Macmillan & Co., New York, 1917).

Seymour, C., The Intimate Papers of Colonel House, Vol. I (Houghton Mifflin Co., Boston and New York, 1926-1928).

Sherman, General W. T., Memoirs (D. Appleton & Co., New York, 1886).

Smith, Justin H., The War with Mexico, 2 vols. (The Macmillan Co., New York, 1919).

Stuart, Graham H., Latin America and the United States (The Century Company, 1928).

Tansill, Charles C., War Powers of the President of the United States with Special Reference to the Beginning of Hostilities, Political Science Quarterly, March, 1930.

Ward, Sir Adolphus, and Gooch, G. R., Cambridge History of British Foreign Policy, Vol. II (The Cambridge University Press, 1922).

Wheaton, Henry, Elements of International Law, 5th English Edition (Baker, Voorhis & Co., 1916).

Willoughby, W. W., Willoughby on the Constitution, Vol. I (1929).

Wilson, George G., Handbook on International Law (West Publishing Co., St. Paul, Minn., 1927).

Wilson, Henry Lane, Diplomatic Episodes in Mexico, Belgium and Chile (Doubleday Page & Co., Garden City, N. Y., 1927).

Wright, Philip Q., The Control of American Foreign Relations (The Macmillan Co., 1922).

B. Periodicals and Newspapers.

Alsberg, Henry G., Mexico: The Price of Recognition, Nation (May 10, 1922).

American Journal of International Law, Vol. XIV, p. 499 (Oct. 1920).

American Journal of International Law, Vol. XVII, p. 742 (Oct. 1923).

American Journal of International Law, Vol. X, pp. 357-367.

American Journal of International Law, pp. 164-166 (March 1925).

Beale, C., Dwight Morrow Agrees With Mexico, The Nation (Jan. 25, 1928).

British Year Book of International Law, p. 57 (1921-1922).

Carranza Wins Recognition at Last as Ruler of Mexico, Current Opinion (Nov. 1915).

Causes of Revolution in Mexico, Unpopular Review (April 1915).

Cornell Law Quarterly, Russia's Government in Bar Courts (Dec. 1925).

Current History, p. 460 (Dec. 1920).

Current History, p. 532 (June 1921).

Current History, p. 711 (July 1921).

Current History, pp. 331-334 (June 1926).

De La Huerta Tells Hughes of Mexico, New York Times (July 19, 1923).

Does Big Business Want Intervention in Mexico? Current Opinion (Aug. 1916).

From Diaz to Carranza, American Review of Reviews (Feb. 1916).

Gamio, Manuel, Emilio Portes Gil—Mexico's New President, Current History (March 1929).

Harvard Law Review, Vol. XXXV, p. 607 (March 1922).

Harvard Law Review, Vol. XXXVIII, p. 816.

Michigan Law Review, Vol. XVIII, p. 531 (1919-1920).

Michigan Law Review, Vol. XXI, p. 789 (1922-1923).

Michigan Law Review, Vol. XXII, pp. 37-39.
Minnesota Law Review, Vol. IX, p. 1 (1924-1925).
Mexican Government Should be Recognized, American Federationist (March 1922).
Mexican Problems, Outlook (Oct. 20, 1915).
Mexico and Recognition, Financial Review of Reviews (Sept. 1922).
Mexico Qualifying for Recognition, New York Times Current History (Aug. 1922).
Mexico Still Fails to Meet Our Terms, New York Times (July 21, 1922, p. 10).
Mexico: Why Not Recognized? New Republic (May 24, 1922).
Obregon Declares for Waiting Policy, New York Times (Sept. 2, 1922).
Oil and Intervention in Mexico, Nation (April 12, 1919).
Our Duty in Mexican Disorder, Literary Digest (Sept. 21, 1912).
Our Duty in Mexico, Independent (Jan. 25, 1915).
Our Policy towards Mexico, Ogg, Frederic A., Munsey's Magazine (May 1911).
Our Oil Victory in Mexico, Literary Digest (Dec. 10, 1927).
Recognition of Mexico by the United States, Pan American Magazine (Oct. 1922).
Sees Mexico Evasive, Washington Post (Aug. 11, 1922, p. 1).
Unhappy Mexico: America's Responsibility, Outlook (Dec. 2, 1914).
What Obregon's Election Means, Literary Digest (July 14, 1928).
Where the Killing of Obregon Leaves Mexico, Literary Digest (July 28, 1928).
Yale Law Journal, Vol. XXVI, p. 339 (1916-1917).
Yale Law Journal, Vol. XXXI, p. 534 (1921-1922).
Yale Law Journal, Vol. XXXIV, p. 499 (March 1925).

INDEX

INDEX 119

occupied by U. S., 90; U. S. withdrawal, 92; Carranza government headquarters, 92.
Vienna, Congress of, 39.
Villa, Francisco, 90; revolt of, 91, 92, 93.

Ward, Sir Dolphus, 38.
Warren, Charles B., 96.
Washington, George, 14, 18, 20.
Webster, Daniel, 20.
West Indies, Spanish, 25.
West, V. J., 103.
Wharton, William H., 43.
Willoughby, W. W., 16, 17.

Wilson, G. G., 11.
Wilson, Henry Lane, 22, 43, 84, 86, 87, 88, 89.
Wilson, Woodrow, 22, 85; hands-off policy, 87, 88, 90, 91, 92, 93; policy toward Obregón, 94, 102, 103.
Wright, Quincy, 7.

Yucatan, 25.

Zamalona, 82.
Zozoya, 36.
Zuloaga, 48.